STANDPOINTS ON GLOBALIZATION AND DECENTRALIZATION

About the Editors

Prof. Ganapathi Palanithurai, Coordinator in Rajiv Gandhi Chair, Gandhigram Rural Institute, presently heads the Department of Political Science and Development Administration, in Gandhigram Rural University, Tamil Nadu. He is also Associated with Centre Planning Commission, State Planning Commission of Tamil Nadu, Population Foundation of India, Ford Foundation, UNICEF, Rajiv Gandhi Foundation, CAPART, Ministry of Rural Areas and Employment and DANIDA (Danish International Development Assistance) in specific areas of activities in connection with empowerment of people.

Prof. Palanithurai has to his credit twenty-nine books and seventy-five articles on three major areas, namely, legislative behaviour, ethnicity and Panchayati Raj system. He was recipient of Fellowship from Sastri Indo-Canadian Institute, New Delhi and World Academy of Art and Science, USA. He is the Chairman of the Tamil Nadu Council for Sustainable Livelihoods. He was a visiting fellow in the MiGill University, Canada in 1989. He is a member of the expert committee constituted by the Government of Tamil Nadu to monitor the training programme for local body leaders.

R. Ramesh is currently working as a Research Coordinator at Rajiv Gandhi Chair for Panchayati Raj Studies in the Gandhigram Rural University, Tamil Nadu. He has a PhD degree in Rural Development, and has specialized in 'Community-Managed Domestic Water Supply System'. He has worked for a variety of projects with varied scope and scale for over 15 years. He won the World Bank's India Country Level Development Marketplace Award—2004 for a proposal on Drinking Water Management. He also served as a Training Expert for a DANIDA assisted project on Water and Sanitation. He worked, for a brief period, as a Project Officer at the India Programme Office of the TdH-NL—a Netherlands based funding agency working on child rights. He has to his credit several articles published in national and international journals of repute. Also, he has co-authored two books namely, *Analyzing Community Problems—Tentacles of PRA Methodology*, and *Globalization: Issues at the Grassroots.*

Standpoints

On Globalization and Decentralization

G. Palanithurai
R. Ramesh

CONCEPT PUBLISHING COMPANY, NEW DELHI-110 059

Cataloging in Publication Data—DK
Courtesy: D.K. Agencies (P) Ltd. <docinfo@dkagencies.com>

Standpoints on globalization and decentralization / [edited by] G. Palanithurai, R. Ramesh.
p. cm.
Interviews of eighteen individuals from India, who have rich knowledge, experience and are active in the field of globalization and decentralization.
Includes index.
ISBN 13: 9788180694783
ISBN 10: 818069478X

1. Decentralization in government—India—Miscellanea. 2. Globalization—India—Miscellanea. 3. Rural development—India—Miscellanea. 4. Scholars—India—Interviews. I. Palanithurai, G. (Ganapathy), 1953- II. Ramesh, R.

DDC 352.283 095 4 22

ISBN 13: 978-81-8069-478-3
ISBN 10: 81-8069-478-X

First Published 2009

Published and Printed by
Ashok Kumar Mittal
Concept Publishing Company
A/15-16, Commercial Block, Mohan Garden
New Delhi-110 059 (INDIA)

Phones : 25351460, 25351794
Fax : 091-11-25357103
Email : publishing@conceptpub.com

Preface

That the subject globalization is divisive and the issues it brings forth are contentious is not new. I shall add that it becomes still more litigious when it is spoken concurrently with decentralization. No two social scientists interprets a phenomenon or a set of data exactly similarly. This variation in interpretations, counter-interpretations, and 'interpretations of interpretations', apparently, stem from the disciplinary choice one has made, ideology one grows up with, or the kind of theoretical framework one deliberately chooses to appraise a phenomenon.

It goes to explain that social scientists, political scientists or economists for that matter look at a phenomenon with his/her 'viewfinder' on. Therefore, consciously or unconsciously one tends to understand and interpret things the way one has learnt to develop a world view. This gives them a standpoint to view and appraise things. Based on standpoints, perceptions and reasoning change. Based on standpoints views differ—and the details one assembles to put up an argument differ. For a researcher, the more the standpoints, multiple are the perspectives developed. Multiple perspectives results in better comprehension of a given phenomenon and more light on the range of issues associated with it.

The 'standpoints'—I mean this slim volume you have in hand—brings to you an array of viewpoints—all diverse. Some positive and very much convincing; some negative equally convincing. There is a third category that keeps in equilibrium and leaves us with a note of caution. As mentioned already the basis for these statements could be realism, pragmatism or empiricism. They draw examples from various rural sectors such as water, agriculture, food security, rural artisans, plantation sector and so on. However, all the statements made here cannot be said as bedrock of observations. It is possible some of the views expressed here could be gut-feeling without sufficient empirical verification. As I do not know the basis for these arguments, at best I consider them as 'sixth sense' of a gamut of highly learnt persons in India. These stalwarts come from diverse backgrounds including Indian Administrative Service, top class academic-cum-research institutions, and social activists' movements. These 'standpoints' have been published in the newsletter: 'Global and Local' brought out as a bi-monthly from the Rajiv Gandhi Chair for Panchayati Raj Studies, GRU, Gandhigram with the support of the Ford Foundation, New Delhi. This is published as a compendium for the benefit of some of the NGOs we have noticed holding one-sided view of globalization, young researchers in political and social sciences to develop their understanding and for the general readers who are interested in the debate on globalization and decentralization.

I think it would not be inappropriate here, if I say that for our research studies on 'Globalization and Decentralization' (look up third wrapper for a list) we have drawn several hypotheses from these views and empirically verified them. Although diverse are the views expressed—as far as decentralization is concerned, except one or two of them—almost all the stalwarts seem to hold a view that local bodies could be a potential institution to challenge the ill-effects of globalization and to make use of the opportunities, if any, brought about by globalization.

I appreciate my research team—Dr. K. Pandimuruga Chinnan, Sri P. Selvamani and Ms. B. Punitha Lakshmi—for meticulously recording these views and the Concept Publishing Company for bringing out this compendium for a wider readership.

G. Palanithurai

Contents

List of Contributors

A.K. Venkatasubramaniam, I.A.S., (Retd.), The Catalyst Trust, No.3, Shanthi Venue, Dr. Radhakrishnan Nagar, Thiruvanmyur, Chennai-41
catalyst_trust@eth.net.in

Chandrika Sharma, Executive Secretary, International Collective in Support of Fishworkers (ICSF), Chennai.

J. Paul Baskar, Chairman, Peace Trust, Near Police Colony, Tricy Road, Dindigul-624005
peacetrust@vsnl.com

M.R. Rajagopalan, Secretary, Gandhigram Trust, Dindigul Distirct, Tamil Nadu
ggmtrust@sify.com

N. Rangaswamy Reddy, Deputy Director (Extension), Coffee Board, No.12, Govindasamy Layout, Sivananda Colony, Coimbatore-641 012, Tamil Nadu
ddecbcbe@sancharnet.in, angadi_reddy@yahoo.co.in

N. Sethuramaswami, Head Draughting Officer, PWD (Retd.), Consultant-Arbitration & Contracts, New 233, Old 91/3, Konnur High Road, Ayanpuram, Chennai- 600 023
sethuramaswami@yahoo.co.in

O. Fernandes, Director, HRF, No.10, Thomas Nagar, Littlemount, Saidapet, Chennai-600 015, Tamil Nadu
hrf@md3.vsnl.net.in

Pradeep Sukumar, Assistant Secretary, The Planters Association Tamil Nadu (PAT), 42 (Old No.67), A.T.T. Colony, Coimbatore-641 018
planterstn@vsnl.net

Raja J. Chelliah, The Chairman, Madras School of Economics, (Behind Data Centre), Gandhi Mandapam Road, Chennai-600 025. Tamil Nadu
rajachelliah@mse.ac.in

R.K. Sivanappan, Member, State Planning Commission, 'Ezhilagam', Chepauk, Chennai-600 005
sivanappan@hotmail.com

S. Muthukumaran, Former Vice-Chancellor, T61/A, 32nd Cross Street, Besant Nagar, Chennai-600090
vsmuthukumaran@yahoo.com

S. Janakarajan, Professor, MIDS, 79, 2nd Main Road, Gandhinagar, Adyar, Chennai-600 020
janak@mids.ac.in

S.S. Meenakshisundaram, Visiting Professor, Rural Development & Decentralization, National Institute of Advanced Studies, Indian Institute of Science Campus, Bangalore-560 012
ssms@nias.iisc.ernet.in

Vibha Gupta, Chairperson, Magan Sangrahalaya Samiti, Wardha-442 001, Maharashtra
vibha@womentech.org

V. Balakrishnan, Convener, Tamil Nadu Primary School Improvement Campaign—TanPIC, #23, Jeyaram Street, Vasanth Apartments 'D', Kuppam Beach Road, Thiruvanmiyur, Chennai-600041
cwdrindia@yahoo.com

V. Jeevanantham, President, Tamil Nadu Green Movement, Nalantha Hospital, 45, Kalaimagal Road, Erode.

V. Vivekanandan, Chief Executive, South India Federation of Fishermen Societies (SIFFS), Trivandrum.

Y. David, People's Education and Action for Liberalization (PEAL), #2, 3rd Street, Maruthupandiyan Nagar, Narimedu, Madurai-625 002, Tamil Nadu
pealmdu@nth.net

1

S.S. Meenakshisundaram

Former Secretary to Government of India
Rural Development Ministry

Decentralization is the direct and faster route to address the issues that globalization brings about. Making proper use of globalization requires access to data and information by the Panchayati Raj Institutions who should be in a position to disseminate it to rural community.

Q: What is your general impression of globalization?

Globalization, I would say, aims at getting the best possible solution in every situation. Globalization brings with it the advantages of producing quality goods at competitive prices. It leads to taking prudent decisions on how to use, in the best possible manner, the natural resources and the skills available in a given economy. Globalization puts into practice the old adage: 'think globally and act locally'. It provides connectivity and saves time instead of trying to reinvent the wheel.

Q: There are people arguing that India has several things to lose in the wake of globalization than the benefits that it would bring. What have you to tell them sir?

One must learn to see the advantages and opportunities globalization would bring. It would bring new ideas, new knowledge, quality goods, competitive spirit and ways to make the best use of the resources available here. Learning to adapt to new economic and market environment is all that is required. It is on our prudence and common sense to decide which one to adopt, where and when. In addition, our entrepreneurs and technicians would come to know who does better what and go for a kind of reverse engineering.

Q: If we take one specific issue, such as commercial drawal of water for example, they say it is going to lead to a serious environmental stress. What do you say about it?

First of all, this is not an issue pertaining to globalization. Over extraction of ground water is something to do with the laws relating to extraction of ground water in this country. To my knowledge there is no legislation to control ground water extraction in several parts of India. Privatization without effective support of law can, in certain cases, lead to harmful effects. We need laws to control over-extraction in the first place, and secondly, effective linkage with rainwater harvesting structures to effect ground water recharge. Now, the situation is anybody can go about digging any number of borewells. This needs to be regulated locally and it has nothing to do with globalization of economy.

Q: How would you react to the argument that globalization would widen the 'rich-poor-divide?'

Not only in India—the rich and the poor have always been there in the society world over. The argument that globalization would widen this gap only sounds cynical and pessimistic to me. Globalization is a gateway of opportunities. It brings several advantages with it. Count the blessings. Take what is useful to you. Keep away from what is not desirable to you.

Q: Who do you think would be benefited the most out of globalization?

It might initially appear that it would benefit only the knowledgeable and the rich. But, in the long run it has to benefit everyone including the poor. It would benefit everyone who can find methods of using it to enhance the quality of work and local products.

Q: What do you think is the role of Panchayati Raj Institutions in facing globalization?

I think decentralization is the direct and faster route to address issues that globalization brings about. Making proper use of globalization requires access to data and information, which the Panchayati Raj Institutions should be in a position to offer to rural communities through Village Information Centres as is attempted by MSSRF. Once this is done and the rural people are equipped with the knowledge to make use of globalization in their best interest, then all the cynicism would disappear. It might take a little time. But, it is the responsibility of the Panchayati Raj Institutions to provide the required leadership and prepare people towards this.

2

Raja J. Chelliah

Chairman
Madras School of Economics, Chennai

Globalization does benefit everybody, or it benefits some more than the others in the short-run. But that depends more on our internal policies. To bring about proportionate growth, you may have to put restrictions—on globalization and the methods of growth inside—for which WTO rules have made provisions. We must understand that much of it is Indian only.

Q: About Globalization, some say, it is stimulating and creative; and others say it is frightening and destructive. What is your view about it?

One thing that many people are worried about is the impact of globalization on the poor and the poor countries. The radicals say that the WTO is going to ruin the poor and the poor countries. If you are not careful and if you are not prepared for it, there is danger in globalization. But as far as India is concerned I can say we are slow, and it is good we are slow. Many people seem to mix up globalization with modernization and mechanization and complain that WTO is completely neglectful of the poor. That is not correct. We need to distinguish.

Q: They say that the impact of integration of world into one economy might affect the autonomy of various countries, what do you say about it?

No country has developed without trade. You can remain a closed economy and stagnate. You have to examine the existing regulations and the policy stand within the country before you go for liberalization. Unless we interfere policy-wise there will not be distributive justice. So, I say it is more internal. Some deliberate restrictions can be placed on what they can do. For instance, in order to liberalize you cut down barriers. But how much to cut down, what to cut down, and where to stop are some of the questions. If these questions were addressed based on hasty and imprudent decisions, your economy will be thrown out of gear. Similarly, your negotiations must be backed with wise domestic action in terms of preparedness for competitiveness.

Q: They say there is no way the poor can benefit from globalization. It is meant only for the rich business giants and the knowledgeable in any country. What have you to tell them?

You must understand that in economic changes, in the short run, there are gainers and losers. For instance, as a result of globalization if some of the Indian companies or foreign companies in India employed 20,000 personnel with fat salaries, those 20,000 people are not going to eat currency. They will spend. They will spend on rice, spend on vegetables, spend on cereals and pulses, and on all kinds of domestic requirements. It will be employment to your farmers, income to the local retailers, income to your Government in terms of sales tax, income tax, service tax etc. The tax (at least 30% of it) is going to be spent for social development causes again. So, ultimately the benefits will go to the production of all commodities. One should study this chain effect instead of taking a surface view of a phenomenon.

Q: Regarding water being made as a 'tradable commodity' by foreign companies in India, there is a great concern raised that it would cause a lot of environmental damage and so on. What is your view about it?

It is true water is a precious resource. It must be managed judiciously. But your reference of damage to the environment and pollution, Indian companies themselves can do as much damage. Usually those in business do not bother how their activities affect environment. This is true of foreigners, Indians and everybody in business. Your country does not have regulations or does not enforce regulations. That's all I would say. FDI in retail trade is also opposed on the grounds that they would throw out small retailers unemployed. But, are not many Indian companies (such as Spenser Plaza, Food World) not doing as much damage to our retailers? This is all again internal.

Q: What do you think are the achievements of globalization so far?

Beginning 1940, until 1990 you were always having Balance of Payment problem. Every year we had Aid India Consortium meeting in Paris where under the auspicious of the World Bank, all friendly governments used to come and pledge aid to poor India. That is all gone now. No BoP problem. The extent of external borrowings has come down tremendously. That means we are free—every citizen is free. Moreover, we can expect a level playing field—be it WTO negotiation or opposing globalization wherever it is affecting badly—only when you are free from debts and independent. It is only now you have really got freedom.

Q: Can 'decentralization' be a response, as far as protection of the interests of the rural livelihoods is concerned?

Yes. They can. I find even women Village *Panchayat* Presidents and *Dalit* persons becoming key persons in the Decentralization system. It is good. But PRIs require constant education and Capacity Building. Then they can voice opinions, fight to get the State and Central Governments to do the right things.

3

Thiru A.K.Venkatasubramaniam

IAS (Retd.)

Managing Trustee of Catalyst Trust
Chennai

Any globalization negotiation besides economic viability, should consider the non-economic parameters such as ethical tenability and environmental sustainability. All that the NGOs and Local Institutions can do is to put the facts before the people. Let the people decide what they should pick up and what they should discard.

Q: The views about and the reactions to globalization are mixed, what is your impression about it?

Globalization has always been there. Trade has always been there. India never remained a closed economy. The form of globalization WTO pushes through is what some people are not comfortable with. They think globalization promotes monoculture in place of variety. They think globalization is a threat to the local culture. But I would say it is parochialism that makes people say it is absolutely no good. We must take a value-neutral view of things. I would attest if some people said that it overrides everything else and puts economic parameters as the prime measure of development. The way it is, it is true this is being one-dimensional. The prime concern seems to be economic viability—plainly 'profitability' which is no good. There are non-economic parameters that are equally important too, which is not in the purview of WTO's scheme of things.

However, it is upto us to make beneficial use of it and keep away from those we think are not suitable or detrimental to us.

Q: Can you elaborate, how do you take value-neutral view of things?

I am talking against taking a narrow outlook or range. Globalization has a tendency to think big, plan big, and act big. Globalization is about opening up instead of insulating ourselves. Think big without destroying the small, is the challenge we should be ready to take in the process of signing in for globalization. How to make use of technology without our becoming subordinate to technology is the challenge we should be prepared to take. How do we balance these things is the real task before us. We should be able to decide what is necessary where, taking essentially into account the larger interest of vulnerable people, rather than taking into consideration the economic merit of things alone.

Q: You say globalization is being uni-dimensional, or that it takes into account only economic merit of things, what do you think is a holistic view of things?

I mean in the context of globalization economic criteria outweighs all other parameters. Why I say this is, take for example, the talk about Expansion of Chennai Meenampakkam Airport. It is argued that Chennai Airport needs to be expanded so that jumbo type aircrafts can also land here. It would bring in business and finance to Tamil Nadu. What is discounted here is the large number of poor people who are living on the outer edge of the airport who will have to be evicted so as to expand the airport. People who fly want the expansion. Their dream is to have facilities in Chennai airport on a par with the airport in Singapore or Washington. What doesn't come in their sight is the vulnerable people who live on the airport periphery in Chennai that they would be rendered homeless and that they are already terrified on hearing about the expansion plan. May be, they have certain magical resettlement plan.

But still, life is distressed. The livelihood source they have established is troubled. Therefore, any globalization negotiation besides economic viability, should consider the following non-economic parameters as well: (i) Is the deal ethically tenable? (ii) Is it technologically feasible? and (iii) Is it environmentally sustainable? In the current scheme of things these three parameters take back seat which is causing all sorts of disorder and societal upheaval.

Q: What do you think globalization has achieved for India, so far?

Globalization of capital is one great thing that has happened. International investors have arrived in Chennai. Global exchange of information is mind-boggling; Exchange of health services is tremendous. Chennai has come to be called the Mecca of Medical facilities. The banking and insurance services in India after the entry of global players have grown wonderfully beneficial to a vast majority of the population. So much so, by globalization it is not only, we liberally open up our gates for foreign trade into India. It is about firmly routed on the ground and at the same time being able to keep the head sky-high. It follows that Indian business also is allowed to flourish in other countries. For example, Hotel Saravana Bhavan, New Delhi is no more news. After globalization, Hotel Saravana Bhavan has started operating in New York and Dubai also. Our Reliance, Tatas and Birlas are firmly gaining ground in other countries in several sectors of business. Micro Soft from the US and the Tatas are making our rural mass computer literates, which is going to be another revolution in information and knowledge explosion for the benefit of the rural masses.

Q: What do you think we should do to make globalization beneficial to rural masses and to protect our villages from being exploited of rural livelihoods?

Globalization in any form—be it modernization or introduction/improvisation of technology—should benefit the rural community and crafts persons who are traditionally involved in related occupations. It should not be allowed to be hijacked by vested interests for private profits. I mention this because it has already happened in the Handloom Sector. The improvisation brought about in weaving sector benefits more the private profiteering interests displacing the traditional handloom weavers for whom it should have been claimable something like a riparian right. So, modernization and technology that should have meant better standards of living of handloom weavers have become rival that challenges their very existence.

Q: What do you think can be the best medium to take globalization message to the rural masses?

Next to TV and newspapers, it is the Village Panchayats that we need to pay our attention to. Although Tamil Nadu Panchayati Raj Act is not the best one in the country, we can feel happy that it is constitutionally recognized and functionally noticeable. Considering the decision-making and financial powers that rest with the Village Panchayats in Tamil Nadu, one can say Village Panchayats have done noticeably well. Therefore, if our concern is protecting rural livelihoods then we need to pitch our efforts in educating the Panchayats and making especially the Village Panchayats aware of various ramifications of globalization that they should be careful about. So, all that we can do is put the facts before people. Let the people decide what they should pick up and what they should discard. We must understand that everything ultimately boils down to human autonomy.

4

M.R. Rajagopalan

Secretary, Gandhigram Trust

Globalization and free market capitalism (liberalization) would bring about the spectacle of unprecedented 'prosperity' and 'economic growth' in a land of degraded farms, forests, ecosystems, and watersheds, failing families and perishing communities. Call these as achievements, if you would.

Q: What is your general impression with regard to globalization of economy?

To make men equal there was a slogan: Liberty, equality and fraternity. To make men unequal, now the slogan is privatization, liberalization and globalization. The term globalization implies that we look at the entire globe—i.e., all the nations as a single entity. This also implies that we transcend nationalism—in which we look at the interests of a particular nation. If we could really establish a world government, which looks after the interests of all humanity—the differences between the rich and the poor, between political, religious groups etc. subsumed—it would indeed be something very good.

Unfortunately, the word globalization as it is being applied in the present context is a brainchild of the Transnational or Multinational corporations (MNCs or TNCs). Most of these TNCs are US based. They made small beginnings in the late fifties grew and flourished in the sixties, seventies and eighties and since the nineties they are aiming to control the finances of the world. Today they have started dictating terms. They do not respect any national frontiers or laws. To my knowledge, globalization is not the wish of any Parliament of any country anywhere in the world. Nor has any UN body said anything in support of it. Globalization is promoted by MNCs in their own interest.

Q: Who, in your opinion, would benefit the most due to globalization?

MRR: Only MNCs would benefit. Let me explain it this way: A sort of moral and economic absurdity exists for the sake of allegedly 'free' market, the single principle: 'commodities will be produced wherever they can be produced at the lowest cost, and consumed wherever they will bring the highest price'. The free market brings in an inequality—the free market is freest to those who have the most money, and is not free at all to those with little or no money, almost for example, as a large corporation 'freely' competing against local, privately owned businesses, has virtually all the freedom, and its small competitors virtually none.

Q: What do you think would be the place of handloom industry when the Indian market is opened up for global players in textiles?

MRR: Even within India handlooms are struggling not being able to compete with the powerlooms and the mill sector. Powerloom goods very substantially get passed as handloom products. At least in Tamil Nadu we could see labour movement from handlooms to powerlooms and to the mill sector for better wages. They have certain livelihood security due to occupational diversification. But, in States like West Bengal, Uttar Pradesh and Andhra Pradesh where especially the handloom weavers do not diversify their search for employment it would be death if it is opened up for MNCs.

Q: Given the trend the process of globalization indicates, what do you think would be the place of handloom industry in the days to come?

MRR: Handloom weavers all over India are mostly in the age group of above forties only. These days, opportunities are plenty and so no youth by choice would not take up handloom weaving as an intelligible livelihood proposition given the amount of drudgery involved in it. He is after employment in the mill sector and young girls would prefer to work as sales girls in cloth stores or sit in STD booths. Ultimately what matters is if one is able to make a decent living. Better technologies should evolve to reduce drudgery and improve productivity and not to replace man. Therefore, I do not see anything wrong if handloom wéavers shift to powerlooms for better wages. These can be taken as part of evolution and growth. Although the market space for handloom goods seems to be reducing, there is scope for handlooms to flourish in some artistic designs like *Kancheepuram, Banaras, Bengal, Patola* etc. verities of *sarees* and others.

Q: What do you think is going to be the achievement of globalization?

MRR: One of the effects of globalization would be these MNCs have a tendency to give high salaries to a small number of professionals who work for them which results in local inflationary tendency. It would affect the common man and the poor, widening the gulf between the rich and the poor.

The globalization and free market capitalism (liberalization) would bring about the spectacle of unprecedented 'prosperity' and 'economic growth' in a land of degraded farms, forests, ecosystems, and watersheds, failing families and perishing communities. Call these as achievements, if you would.

5

R.K. Sivanappan

Member
State Planning Commission, Tamil Nadu

Going by surface and ground water potential in India, India should not face water scarcity for another 40-50 years at least. It is absence of proper water conservation, harvesting and management practices in Indian Agriculture that is causing all the scarcity.

Q: Member of the State Planning Commission, what do you think, the Government and the Indian farmers should do to be able to survive in the global competition?

Given the size of Indian population that India is self-sufficient in food production is a good indicator of Indian Agriculture doing well. India needs to do better in the wake of globalization. It can do better provided we carry out certain activities in terms of 'Domestic Preparedness'. By domestic preparedness I mean, concentrating on land productivity, water productivity, putting in place appropriate water management technologies and practice, making the outcome of agricultural research reach the farmers, preventing river water and ground water being polluted by industrial effluents and municipal sewage water.

Q: Can you elaborate it a little?

Take for example, paddy cultivation. At the moment the intensity of cultivation is only about 130 per cent and it can be increased upto 300 per cent as we have sunshine for 365 days. But the main constraint is water. At the same time we are using only about 25 per cent of surface water flow, meaning water wasted by allowing into the sea. Tamil Nadu is struggling to get 205 TMC water from Karnataka, whereas in actuality not less than 2000 TMC is wasted by allowing into the sea in Karnataka itself. Going by the ground water potential and annual rain fall in India, India should not face water scarcity for at least another 40-50 years. In my opinion, the problem of water scarcity in India is man-made. I mean we have not created adequate water harvesting and storage structures. Several of the traditional water harvesting structures and *nullas* are under encroachment and there is no adequate water management system in place in all sectors. These should be taken up first.

Q: With the growing ground water scarcity, and emerging WTO context what do you think is likely to be the future of Indian farmers?

One of the status indicators in an agrarian economy is a farmer with irrigation facility is rich and a farmer with dryland/rainfed land is poor. So, water is one main dividing line between the rich and the poor in Indian villages. Green Revolution in my opinion, and in the opinion of many, benefited the irrigated agriculture only. Another fact is that the Department of Agriculture of the Government has, often, acted like Department of Agriculture hyphen 'Irrigated Land'. There should be Second Green Revolution initiated focusing specially on dryland agriculture. There is 38-40 million hectares of cultivable waste, fallow and waste land which can be brought under cultivation. I am happy to note that the honourable Prime Minister talked about Second Green Revolution through rainfed/drylands.

Q: Generally, pursuits in Agriculture are viewed as non-profitable, what is your reaction to it?

In countries like Israel, both surface and ground water is a property of the State. In India owner of a given piece of land owns the water below the ground. He can use it. He can misuse it. He can mismanage it. They do not bother to understand the need for water management. Pursuits in agriculture are not profitable to those who do not consider the importance of water management. There are methods and techniques such as SRI which tells how to reduce irrigation by 40 per cent while at the same time increase paddy production by about 30 per cent which our farmers should adopt. This is increasing productivity per unit area. This is done in sugarcane cultivation by many farmers in Erode and Sivagangai districts, where they report 2.5 times more production. It is profitable. The farmers need to be a little more intelligent and there is need for training and demonstration to that extent. It is stated that only 5-10 per cent research findings are being adopted in the field.

Q: What do you think should be the role of Local Bodies in promoting rural livelihoods, especially the farm related ones?

For me promoting rural livelihoods largely hinges on the protection of ground water sources and surface water storage structures. One view is that user control system can improve efficiency in water management. The Water Users Associations can also serve the purpose. The Local bodies can help establish users associations. There is Ground Water Regulation Act coming up. The Local Bodies can ensure that the provisions are adhered to at the village level so that indiscriminate draft of ground water is prevented. Similarly, Institutions and Universities should develop convincing demo plots and models. They should also have a system of interacting with Village Panchayats and make their research findings reach the farmers.

6

Y. David

State Convener
Joint Action for Sustainable Livelihoods (JASuL), Madurai

Globalization, in its current form, is no good for the people. It is companies-centred and not people-centred nor is it nature friendly. We need to develop a 'New Generation of Panchayat Functionaries' who would act as a force against the current pattern of globalization.

Q: What, in your opinion, is happening to Agriculture in Tamil Nadu as a corollary of globalization?

This question requires a historical analysis of whatever has happened to agriculture in Tamil Nadu since the British people started directing Indian farmers what our farmers should cultivate and for whose consumption. One example, I can give is about the type of cotton we grew before the British and the type we are growing today which the Britishers left here. Today we are unaware of the original cotton that belonged to India. In 1960s, under the guise of Green Revolution, the Government took over the power of deciding for the farmers what should be cultivated, what fertilizers and pesticides to use and so on. Recently, as a corollary of the culture being promoted by globalization processes, corporate companies (MNCs) tell the farmers what our farmers should cultivate, where to buy the seeds and what fertilizers to apply and so on. In short, so long as farming remained in the hands of the farmers, farming was remunerative and sustainable. Today, we remain labourers in our own farms.

Q: Isn't keeping pace with change—change in technology, change in scientific advancement—development? Clinging on to archaic ways of doing things wouldn't let us remain static?

These are mindsets. For me, development carries weight only when it benefits the people, does not harm nature and is sustainable. For others it could be growth rate—8 per cent or more. Technology is necessary. My contention is when a 'tool' can do, why bring 'machinery'? For instance, we had a tool called 'plough' for ploughing the agricultural fields. It was cheap, locally made, light on the soil and harmless to earthworms. It could have been improved through research. But we replaced it with 'tractors'—machinery. First of all, use of tractor tightens the soil. There are also subsidies given to buy tractors. It promotes tractor sales, and serves the interests of the chain of industrialists who are involved in manufacturing and marketing of tractors. To the farmers it has increased the cost of cultivation. To the wage-earners it has reduced the number of days they get employment in a year. Technology should fill in a human need. Market should not impose things upon me. This is a culture brought about by globalization. This has made us lose our land, water, livestock, forests, and other livelihood resources.

Q: Do you believe that going back to the traditional agricultural practices would be able to feed the growing population of India?

Left uninfluenced, our farmers would go in for production of food-oriented crops only. We would be able to feed everyone in this country 'a food without pesticide-residues'. For this, we should not count on rice or wheat only. We should take into account all forms of cereals and pulses. Another aspect is extraction of soil fertility through indiscriminate use of chemical fertilizers and pesticides have eventually started showing diminishing returns. Use of fertilizers and pesticides has killed the fertility of the soil while at the same time they have caused increase in the cost of input. There are bio-manures and recent technologies such as EMO which are meant for systematic recovery of lands that have lost fertility. I mean traditional farming with modern methods. I am happy natural farming is growing as a movement in Tamil Nadu. It can make our farmers hold their heads high.

Q: What is specifically wrong with globalization?

Most of us in JASuL Network (Joint Action for Sustainable Livelihood) are of the strong opinion that the current pattern of globalization benefits only people 'above upper middle class' in the society. Globalization mystifies several things—one of the prime things being knowledge. Knowledge is mystified, centralized, and commercialized. The kind of development promoted centres around MNCs, and privatization with profit orientation. It does not have people in its focus. Its focus is commerce and companies. It is unethical. Business without ethics is anti-people, anti-nature and anti-god. Hence, the current pattern of globalization needs to change to be in favour of decentralization of political power.

Q: In order to face the challenges brought about by globalization what do you think we need to do?

We need to make local bodies a force against the current pattern of globalization. For this to happen, a new generation of Panchayat functionaries needs to be developed. Today minus some, many of the Village Panchayat functionaries act like contractors of Government machineries such as Block Development Office and the DRDA. We, at JASuL Network, are trying to develop a concept which we call 'Green Panchayats' to protect and promote natural resources and to fight against all obnoxious aspects of globalization.

7

O. Fernandes

Director
Human Rights Advocacy & Research Foundation (HRF)
Chennai-15

There is nothing private about private limited companies in India. You remove public resources from private companies, they would all fall like a bag of pins. They are living on public resources—land, water, road, power supply, bank loan, insurance, tax holiday, our rivers to pump out their effluents...

Q: What is your impression of globalization?

As far as I am concerned, globalization is the highest form of imperialism, whereby in the name of neo-liberal economics it is an effort once again for the world's huge Transnational Corporations to re-dominate and re-control whatever is left of the resources of the poorer countries and their markets. And it is a market of domination and super-exploitation and emasculation of the livelihood of the people. So, there is a long struggle ahead of the marginalized, the poor and the working classes.

Q: Conformists of WTO state that WTO agreements are based on negotiations and that WTO is a democratic forum. How do you react to it?

All those who believe that the WTO is a negotiable forum, is a democratic forum, and every country has one vote is all myth. No decision will ever be taken in the WTO on vote basis. You can never negotiate any equal terms of trade. It is just not possible. It will only be on consensus. This consensus is between the large industrialized countries *vis-à-vis* the fast developing countries—such as India, China, Argentina, Venezuela etc.

Q: Perhaps, you closely observed the WTO Ministerial meeting held at Hong Kong last December? What have you to tell about it?

India played a very dirty role in the WTO negotiations. The Commerce Minister for India said that India was a good broker in the Hong Kong meeting. He meant there was an alliance of about 140 countries and India broke that alliance. They were pushing at least the GATS—the services sector out of the WTO discussion. India broke that. India breaking it was understood because the Indian state represents the big capitalists' interests in the country. But Brazil was a workers party. That very clearly shows that capitalism today is so powerful that it penetrates even the workers party. You push Brazil into position and there is nothing to negotiate excepting to believe that if they want to survive then they must be friends of this industrialists countries. There is no conflicting role. The only country that did fight to some extent was Venezuela, and a few other countries did fight. The industrialized countries said that they would cut down the subsidies by 2013. But that is a fraud. They would remove what is the most important in the green box and then in the green box they will not cut the subsidies.

Q: But, why do you think India does this? Aren't the people in power aware that the toiling class, as you say, would be affected?

It's because the Government represents those interests. It is not a Government of the people. It is a Government of the capitalists' interests. WTO is actually the voice of the TNCs. The left movement never put up a united voice for the people to believe in, and that's where globalization is scoring in India. If the different fractions of the broad left movement can speak with one voice, the WTO would have had a very difficult time in India.

Another example that can show how the Government represents only the capitalists' interests is the taxation policy. India's luxury taxes are the lowest in the whole world today. So, where do you get your revenue from? You are refusing to tax the rich. You look up the political manifesto of the leading political parties today. There is nothing to say about the impact of globalization on livelihoods; there is nothing to say about regeneration of agriculture or irrigation facilities. Then whose interests does the Government represent.

Q: They say privatization can bring inefficiency and the most needed finance which can boost the economy. What have you to say about it?

You see there is nothing private about private limited companies in India. You remove public resources from private companies, they would all fall like a bag of pins. They all are living on public money. You call it a SIPCOT. Who has started business there? All huge MNCs. You build them infrastructure and build them roads without charging them Re.1, then you give them water; then you subsidize electricity payment for them; then you give them a gestation period for tax—call it tax holiday. To draw water you give them place and to pump out effluents, you give them our rivers. They take loans from your banks. They take insurance cover. It is a loot of public resources. What I call national wealth. It is a loot of national wealth by the private sector which the State has presided over and legitimized.

Q: This Newsletter we are interviewing you for, has 'Food Security' as the focus. What do you think is the state of food security in the wake of globalization?

Don't limit food security to PDS. We are all surviving because of the existence of informal markets. There is still informal economy in our country working. The rest still they have to go to the open market only. We don't depend on formal markets. We still have local production going.

We don't have to go to the Bata or Nike to buy shoes. We have local products as well. The poor have some alternatives to get that cheaper. If all of us have to eat in Hotel Saravanabavan all the three times, we are all gone. The point is we must strengthen the informal markets. There is a vast majority of the poor—both in rural and urban areas who depend on these informal markets. Toiling people—they are finding it difficult to survive this globalization.

Q: Panchayats as the Constitutional Government close to the toiling mass, you keep mentioning about what do you think is the place of Panchayats in the context of globalization?

Globalisation means in a way centralizing. Under globalization you are centralizing not merely within the Indián States you are also centralizing it at the world level. So, globalization is a total anti-thesis to decentralization and devolution of power. In my opinion, one organ that will be worst affected because of globalization is the Panchayat. You and I are saying give more financial allocation to Panchayats. Whereas WTO and TNCs are saying cut the finances and the markets must be allowed to operate. So, truth for them becomes false for us. I hear that there are Municipalities in some of the developed countries that say: 'This is a WTO free municipality'. This is WTO free zone. No products coming out of WTO agreements are allowed in side the municipality. Sections 159 and 160 of the Panchayats Act gives the power to the Panchayats the authority to provide 'No Objection Certificates'. TNCs think it restricts their freedom of operation. Now, they are making moves to take away that power.

Q: Do you think the local governments would be able to combat globalization?

I would believe it is possible. The Panchayats in Tamil Nadu have not moved to that stage to associate themselves with other people's movements. That's one of the areas where we need to help them—to associate with women, Dalits, tribals, working class etc. That linkage is not made yet. I think that linkage is very important. If we can work with the Panchayats systematically and push the Government to function more independently, there is a chance of fighting globalization from below.

8

S. Janakarajan

Madras Institute of Development Studies, Chennai

There is no such thing as 'governmental failure'. There could be only lapses, or delays in service delivery. Governmental failure is an expression invented by the advocates of globalization, especially the World Bank, to be able to argue in favour of privatization.

Q: What is your general impression of 'Globalization'?

Globalization. First of all, whose making is it? No country asked for it. It is an imposition upon us and upon all the developing economies of the world. It sends across messages that imply unless you fall in line you will be isolated; and the World Bank would not lend. Globalization would make your country investor friendly. It tends to promote privatization as a general solution to all the problems of governance. In my view globalization is promoted by the World Bank and the IMF influenced by corporates in G7 and G8 nations, most of which are US based. This is imperialism. It comes to us only for ratification and we have no say in it. We need to understand and make our rural community understand that the idea of globalization views India as a marketplace. For those producers in Northern America or Western Europe the sheer size of consumers in India is the attraction.

Q: Sectors are increasingly being privatized in India, what have you to tell about it?

Yes. It is true even some of the Boards of the Government (such as Delhi Jal Board) is being handed over to private operators. In Tamil Nadu, we have New Thiruppur Water Company (BOOT). With the backing of the World Bank 'privatization' is being promoted in India as a way out for all kinds of lapses in service delivery. They call privatization as a solution to 'Governmental failure'. I would not call it 'Governmental failure'. These are 'lapses' or 'problems'. 'Governmental failure' is an expression used by the corporates and the World Bank to be able to argue in favour of privatization. Moreover, privatization cannot be the only answer as it is being promoted. If approach is the problem 'decentralization' could be a viable proposition, and why are we not giving a thought about it. Decentralization with community participation approaches have really worked wonde·s in several Indian villages.

Q: Can you share with the readers of 'Global and Local' your views on trend in the use of ground and surface water in Tamil Nadu after privatization efforts?

Dependence on ground water increased with the introduction of Green Revolution in India. Green Revolution introduced two to three crops in a year which otherwise was one crop a year. This required more water for irrigation, assured irrigation, and it introduced technologies that supported assured irrigation. Pumping ground water through motorized pump sets became essential during the period of Green Revolution. People started paying scant attention to ponds, *nullas* and surface water storage tanks etc. Now, the ground water levels have reached an abysmal state. It is continuously overstressed. Overdraft of ground water has become common place leading to more and more areas being announced as 'critical'. Now we are trying to rediscover the watershed areas. The very expression 'competing demand for water' came into being only after commercial drawal of water began.

Q: Who do you think would benefit the most out of globalization processes?

The price of computers have come down; the price of mobile phones have come down; the interest rates of home loans and price of foreign cars have come down; the price of almost all electronic gadgets have come down. The price of flight tickets have come down by almost half of what it was. The FDI has increased. The Sensex is making records in terms of comfortablity to the investors. You get access to all kinds of paid-channels on the TV. India has the highest number of English speaking people in the world. Aren't we proud of these developments? But, who are the beneficiaries of these products? The top 5 per cent of the population who are moneyed! Globalisation is for them.

I give you another picture. Crop loan is viewed as non-credit worthy and risky by the bankers whereas 'home loans' are sold like products. The cost of agricultural inputs including seeds, pesticides, and fertilizers has increased manyfold; the output price has come down; the cost of pumping ground water for irrigation has gone up; even people in the villages have been pushed to a state of purchasing drinking water for a price. The real income of the farmers has come down. The farmers are fighting for 'support price' unable to get 'a fair price'. There is wide-spread migration from rural areas in search of employment in urban areas. This segment comprises more than 65 per cent. The remaining 30 per cent are middle and upper middle class who would buy a home loan and a two-wheeler and would glide to the end of his life paying the EMI. I have just presented to you the facts that describe three scenarios and I leave the analysis to you.

9

Vibha Gupta

Chairperson, Magan Sangrahalaya Samiti
Wardha

"I am not afraid of the products, nor of the markets. One major thing I am afraid of is the war on our psyche, which silently brings in a kind of inferiority complex or the passivity to accept that the values, technological status, and the intelligentsia that comes from outside are superior to ours. This hurts me more. We must believe that globalization has no meaning if we can uphold strong and self-sustaining footing of this country."

Q: What is your general impression of globalization and what is happening about it in India?

One major thing is this. It's a psychic war. It's a war on your psyche. Once you threaten a society, which is vulnerable that you don't have strength; you don't have capacity to grow; you don't have capability to take hold of your own problems, you can silently attack it. Create a passivity or inferiority complex and carry on your business with that psyche operating in your favour. That psyche is what hurts me more. Globalization is basically, an inferiority complex that the rich countries are giving the poor countries their own values, according to their own technological status, intelligentsia, and creativity. I think that attack has to be addressed. It is not the product. This is a whole psyche saying that Indian products or marketing ethics do not match the world market, so you better change, you become like us, you dress like us, you pose like us, and you become another model or robot as theirs, which I am really afraid that it shouldn't happen. So, the product is not the real issue. That psychic war or submissiveness that it is going to bring, the wrong values that it is going to bring, what are we going to do about it. That's the major issue.

Q: Our concern is more of the social sector. Can you show an example of this psychic hurt in India on the social sector?

I can give you this example. In our country we all face poverty-driven diseases—may be malnutrition, anemia, miscarriages etc. Suddenly we go to life-style diseases—the diseases that come because of life-style—HIV-AIDS, diabetes, cardiac attack, obesity etc. This is because people in America think that these are the major health problems. Suddenly, you drive all your resources into this. All your major tropical diseases such as TB, malaria, filaria, are not looked at, because the big boss is saying that the life-style diseases are the major problems we are going to suffer for. This has killed the total health process of India. We had more or less won the war on leprosy, we were working on TB, we were going to win it, and by that time there was total diversion. Nobody talks about population now. China and India are not looked at as countries with creativity, ethical and ethnic beauty. They are seen as big market places. You don't talk about population now. It does not any more pose a threat. Suddenly, how these values change. You know, that inner tranquility is questioned. That's where I am against globalization—the process of them or anybody else valuing us, and of imposing values on us.

Another example I can give is every small farmer in India used to have small land holdings—one acre, three acres and so on. He was growing four or five varieties of crops as basic foods, vegetables, pulses and so on. He would manage that field—because it is not a market that he was dealing with. It is sustainability he is dealing with. Suddenly you tell him: *'what the non-sense are you doing having small fragmented holdings, put them all together and let's do farming the European style—the mega farming'*.

Finish with small farmers. Where does this agenda come from? This can't be my country's agenda, because this country has always lived with fragmented holdings. People here lived with creative farming and organic farming. Suddenly you have altogether a new agenda coming up. That you give seeds, you give fertilizers, and you would say which of the vegetables or fruits I should grow. You are creating a sleepy country—a country whose psyche and culture is questioned.

Q: What, in your opinion, is the place of traditional artisans as a consequence of globalization?

As far as artisans are concerned, we have lost the war. Artisans are no more the service sector for us. Artisans are basically the cultural sector for us. They are embodied with science or skills as you may call it. How can these people become part of your service sector? We are not taking any technical jump in their traditional know-how. We are not tuning them to the new requirements. On the other side we take away all their resources, all their raw material bases. How can they survive? You no more wear cotton—our weavers are gone. You no more use pottery products—how can the potters survive? He was part of your living. Now you think you don't need them.

Q: How do you think one should look at these issues and go about addressing them?

How to look at globalization here? Is globalization a quality jump—a quantitative jump—or is it a dream jump? (a) We have more of middleclass growing. So, they have different demands. So, cater to their demands. And you have a bigger jump in the economy—is that the agenda? (b) Or you have a country, which is growing many things in such huge quantity for which you need market. So, you become part of the market. (c) What you are producing is of such bad quality automatically good quality will enter the market. Good quality products would definitely take away the bad quality products' market. We have to see what we are addressing. Is it quality or quantity or creation of a new class? If we say we want to address the problems of quality because we really produce very poor quality products. Work on that. Who will work on that? Our technical institutes, our IITs, including Gandhigram you take a sector and improve it. In spite of knowing all techniques the unfortunate thing is we are not working on it. The global economy walks on the assurance so that they get into the market. In the same terms if our Government gives assurance to our producers and gives these assurances, many local producers and artisans will thrive.

Q: Let's get down a little more specific. How can we help potters in a trend where pottery is getting fast sidelined by other products, such as plastics for example?

Constructions are coming up very fast all over. If you are really serious you can use a lot of pottery products in building construction. You can have flooring, you can have tiles, you can have almost everything made by potters in house construction if you really want to support pottery. Even our cooking system, what we are getting into these days is Teflon coated materials, which are toxic. Pottery articles are hygienic and organic. You can use your gas stove no problem. But use pottery articles. It can be a movement. On the one side we are breaking the tradition and we are not making any efforts to revive that tradition. In our place, after Diwali, many of the potters are still left with the 'mud lamps'. Nobody buys them after Diwali. What one Panchayat President did was, he mooted an idea: *See, we have all celebrated Diwali at home. Why don't we all celebrate Dewali one-day at the local temple? All bring twenty, thirty, or fifty lamps; we shall light them at the temple and celebrate a community 'Diwali'*. It was such a vibrating festival with about 2000 lamps shining at one place. So, culturally what has he done? He revived it in a different manner and made it a community thing. That way there is no cultural revival taking place in India. The only cultural revival is mobile phones, or buy a better automobile than you had before. We can really work on cultural revival which sustains traditional livelihoods, and which keeps the community together.

You mentioned about plastics. But as a storage thing earthen pots are very good from health point of view. Of course, you have to have a lighter material to carry water but not to store. Storing water in plastic pot is bad for this country which is already malnourished. Now we have to re-educate the people, showing the science behind it. We never get into the science behind certain cultural practices such as wearing *khadi,* why plastic *bindi* should not be used, why use flower on the head, why store water in earthen pots and so on. There is science behind everyone of this. We need to understand the logistics of all that had been coming with culture. We must find ways to scientifically put it across to people. Thus, we can save some of the traditional industries and artisans.

Q: In this revival exercise, do you find any role for the Government?

The funny thing in our country is we are prepared to tell Japan that they can come here and take away all our iron ore. But, our own artisans don't have a policy that we need to grow 30 per cent of bamboo for our artisans, 20 per cent of these trees would go for carpentry work and so on. All your good quality woods are going for making pulps, making plywood and to the sports industry. There is no demarcation that these artisans will have this stock. Secondly, there is no protection even for people who have to be protected. The Government is withdrawing itself anything that is community based; anything to do with artisans; anything to do with the poor, as if they can't run the country. In order to protect the interests of the jute farmers and jute workers of Bangladesh, that country was able to say: '*We have plenty of jute, no more plastics. Jute must be used as the primary material for any kind of packing'.* Just one single policy all those involved in that sector have been protected and they are selling at massive quantity. Such protective measures are necessary. Chanting that everything has been opened; be in competition; do the best. This will not work for the poor. Here is a sector, which is vulnerable, which has been protected for long by the Government, by landlords, by society and so on. Suddenly you open it and say you die or live we don't have any idea. This is not possible. You have to take care of them. They are suffering because of your wrong policies, unwanted leases, wrong subsidies and tax-holidays you are allowing to the big industries.

Q: What kind of role can we find for Panchayats here?

One is the resource base of that village. They need to plan. Every Panchayat functionary should know what are their assets, land area, rivers, sand, stone, and wood. Then they must go into planning how to make the best use of their resources without allowing others from exploiting them for making private profits. The Panchayats should take care of their own demands, understand it carefully. The Panchayats have to be careful about their market. There should be some kind of a kinship, emotional tie. You can't leave your weavers sleep hungry, you can't let your potters die because of the stupid policies of the State. Unless there is a social bearing in the whole thing you can't mitigate any of these. In all these process of empowerment there has to be an underlying empowerment of our being, of being an Indian, of belonging to this culture, this soil, this society, and this environment. Globalization has no meaning if you have strong self-sustaining footing of this country.

10

Thiru N. Sethuramaswamy

Secretary
Tamil Nadu Visvakarma Artisans Sangam, Chennai

Lion and lamb can roam together anywhere they want; and eat anything they want is the kind of democracy globalization is bringing about.

Q: First of all, is there a clear-cut definition of rural artisans anywhere properly documented?

By conventional definition 'traditional rural artisans' of Tamil Nadu comprise five classes of artisans (the *panchalas*), viz., carpenters, goldsmiths, blacksmith, founders, i.e. workers in metals (brass and copper vessels), and stonesmiths. I would say you can include 'potters' also in this. I wonder how they were missed. Although mention is made about *Viswakarmas* even in *Rig Veda*, to my knowledge the earliest document about them was made in 1805 by a French Priest called Abbe J.A. Dubois in his empirically researched book titled: 'Hindu Manners, Customs and Ceremonies' published from the Oxford. (OUP: 1897). Traditionally these are the five classes of rural artisans known as *Kammalas* in Tamil Nadu. Now, if you conduct a survey it is possible you get several others who might be regionally significant. But, they are all later additions only.

Q: What were their traditional status in the society?

They were the people who used to make everything from plough-share to temple top; from warriors swords to chariots' wheels; and from artistic jewellery to sickle for harvesting. They were in fact the native engineers with skills handed down from generation to generation. One example we can give is of the geometrical perfection in temple-stone-carving when there was absolutely no technology available. During kings periods they were respected, although by caste they were considered to be of very low rank among the *sudras*. The artisans of those days felt no necessity to use many of the tools that European artisans had. One or two axes, as many saws and planes, all of them so rudely fashioned that a European workman would be able to do nothing with them. The working materials of a goldsmith usually comprised a tiny anvil, a crucible, two or three small hammers, and as many files. With such simple tools the patient Indian artisans could produce specimens of work which were often not to be distinguished from those imported at great expense from foreign countries. The status today is we are fighting to be classified under MBC category.

Q: Can you tell what is globalization doing for them?

My understanding of globalization is: 'it is something like saying lion and lamb can roam together anywhere they want; and eat anything they want'. Globalization, as far as the traditional rural artisans are concerned, is further deteriorating the significance of the rural artisans, viz. the goldsmiths, blacksmiths, carpenters, and the vessel makers. It may help the business class and not the artisans like goldsmiths who depend on earning wage out of his capabilities. So, it benefits those who can invest money, and sometimes benefits consumers and it never benefits the producers or artisans who sell their artistic skills and acquired talents. It pressurizes the producers to give the best at the least possible cost, otherwise the market would not be in favour of him. The trend today is better being a trader rather than being a producer or an artisan. Now, all the engineering fields are occupied by others, not by the artisans' generation. The blacksmith dealing with iron lost his entire occupation to major factories; the founders dealing with brass and copper have no orders for production of household utensils because of stainless steel industry; the carpenters struggle to thrive due to the arrival of synthetic products and so on.

Q: Can you elaborate it a little with some examples?

You take the example of jewellery. The trend today is: 'fashion in; quality out'. People are after fashion, design and branded jewellery. They do not seem to bother if they really buy gold when they buy gold. Advertisements such as 'no making charges', 'no wastage' attract them. But they do not stop to think: 'how can a jeweller sell a necklace without charging for the making'? Or I question: Does the jeweller mentions while filing his Income Tax returns that for so many people he paid making charges from his pocket as philanthropy. The machine-cut fashion attracts the consumers, and the customers do not understand that they are cheated in terms of quality of the gold they are delivered. I do not know if you know that wrist watch makers such as the Titan at Hosur have started making fashion jewellery of machine-cut design which is fast emerging as a challenge to the workmanship of the traditional artisans.

Q: You spoke about gold quality. They say hallmark stamps are soon going to be made compulsory?

Yes, it is true, and it must be insisted in order to protect the consumers from being cheated with poor quality material. A rapid survey conducted in 11 popular jewellery showrooms in Chennai revealed that many of them sell sub-standard quality. The funniest part of this is, except one, none of them challenged the results of the survey. I would say even that one jeweller challenged it because it would serve as an advertisement amidst customers who insist on being cheated. Certain shop owners have advertised that they have installed machinery worth a million rupees for instant testing of the quality of gold as against the traditional checking by hand, i.e. by rubbing on the stone. But the menace of cheating the customer with sub-standard quality continues as ever, for a detailed report on this look up Dinakaran dated 09.10.2006.

Q: What kind of trade trend, do you think, is catching up in jewellery business that affects or provides opportunities to the traditional artisans?

I hope you will agree with me in this point that the number of people who go to a goldsmith for making a chain or necklace has come down tremendously. They want to buy instantly at showrooms where they can select from a range of fashions and designs. This has necessitated the goldsmith to be employed for a wage by jewellery shop owners or in jewellery showrooms instead of being self-employed, as he was earlier. But again, this was about the recent past. The current trend is towards branded jewellery where big players from North India (especially Jaipur and West Bengal) and abroad showcase their jewellery designs in the showcase of our showrooms. Our popular jewellery shops are renting out their display windows for fashion jewellery to be displayed. That is somebody else product upon which you have made no investment being displayed in your showroom. The strategy of: '*do business with others money*' is catching up among even the middle class jewellery shop owners. You get a percentage of the profit-trade mentality displacing the artisan. Moreover, Ambal Jewellers I can understand, Valli Vilas Jewellers I can understand, but where do the Khazhana Jewellers come from? There are traders coming in anew, who were never in jewellery making as artisans.

Q: Given the trend jewellery business is in, what do you think is the future of traditional goldsmiths of Tamil Nadu?

Although fashion and branded jewellery seem to be catching up the market with a big bang, it is there in the back of the mind of everyone of us 'the purity of the gold one is buying'. Our traditional jewellers instead of serving as an agent of the branded jewellery should try to promote quality consciousness in buying gold ornaments and make a name for them as being dependable in terms of purity of the gold used. Similarly, the Government should heavily tax the branded jewellery and the gold that comes from other States. The income generated that way can be made use of for allocating to the welfare of the traditional artisans. The Government sponsored Handicrafts Board is nowhere near to help traditional artisans face the challenges. The artisans need a separate 'Traditional Artisans Welfare and Industrial Development Board (TAWID)' at Central and State levels with structures to be of help at the grassroots level as well. Otherwise they cannot face the open competition from lions---the jewellery showroom owners who have recently developed a mindset of viewing jewellery business sons goldsmiths. The lambs (artisans) can cooperate with lions with appropriate safeguards, for which the Government should devise protective measures, one of which could be this TAWID Board.

11

V. Vivekanandan

Chief Executive, SIFFS

I am ready to respect those who critique globalization with a consistent logic. But, I find many of the anti-globalization arguments are based on one-sided deal. If globalization is evaluated only as opening up to the outside world you will get completely contradictory answers. To benefit from globalization, at first, we have to set our home in order.

Q: In the globalization context, what do you think are the major changes taking place in India—especially in the primary sector such as fishery?

I would say fisheries have been relatively open even before 1991, which set of policies we consider as globalization is still tricky sometimes to say. The kind of market changes that are taking place is one thing we can definitely talk about. Even before our current round of globalization, there is enough experience in managing common property resources that market gives wrong signals. Indeed, in fisheries, this is a fact acknowledged world-wide. Especially for primary produces like the ones from agriculture and fishery what we lack in India is collective planning in terms of what we produce and how we sell. It is complete anarchy. It leads to individual decisions resulting in unsustainable practices. The market signals, often in many sectors unless they are moderated and countered by collective decision-making, leads to disaster. You get one technology you get good catch (fish) then, everybody invests in that of net or type of fishing, then you face the problem of over exploitation of fishery resources; or the prices crash. One thing that is very clear if you go by market signals you end up over exploiting the resources. Globalization gives you also the technology to do this.

Q: Aren't advancement of science and technology paramount for the development of any sector?

They are. There is no second opinion about it. What I mean to say is, in fisheries for example we introduced trawling without any mechanism to control trawling. It is the same thing with aquaculture in India. Scientists today will blame the administrators saying that the technology is good, but it had to be managed. But when the technology was introduced which scientist told us that there are limits and that we should not go beyond this limit. No scientist in India ever told us that there are limits when you are introducing trawling—the same green revolution thing. New technology is sold without saying that this is useful but within the certain limits. If you set the limits then people will decide if they want or don't want that technology. Then the Government would also think if it should really support and subsidize such technology. You say it is a great technology. The first ten fellows who use this would become prosperous. After a few years everyone goes for this and then all are in bad shape—worse than before. You have moved your costs higher. You have become more vulnerable. Earlier all you were to do was to starve. Today you go the extent of committing suicide. As long as you have things within your manageable limits, things fall in place.

Q: Who are to be blamed for this? Is it the scientific institutions or the users of technology?

My contention is that a scientist does not know the economics of technology. The economists in the scientific institutions are either useless, or considered as poor cousins. It is like non-technical jobs in a hospital. Social scientists and economists command no respect in a scientific institution. I would say scientific institutions in India have no understanding of socio-economics associated with a technology. You can't blame external world for this. You can't blame the WTO for this and you can't blame IMF for this. Our scientists and technologists know their demo farms only. They do not know the repercussions it will have on the economy as a whole. One plot you do excellent results. If it is spread to ten farms what are the consequences; if it is spread to 100 farms, if it spreads to 1000 farms what are the consequences. They do not even work out a scenario. That is why I say, technology related policy-making is very poor in India. What are you talking of promotion and dissemination in isolation. Do our scientists ever analyze whether a new technology to be introduced is suitable for mass propagation. A lot of problems I would trace to ourselves and not to the rest of the world. If we know what we need then we can manage the rest of the world. Basically from the globalization point of view, we can attribute many of these to taking up only one side of what the developed countries adopt to achieve economic growth and prosperity.

Q: Can you elaborate what do you mean by taking up only one side of a model or one-sided deal?

I mean to say you need certain controls while deregulating. In developed countries in many of these areas, they have very strong controls. It includes other common property—roads for example. There are toughest regulations in terms of how many vehicles with what weight can ply on a road. They use taxation, incentives, disincentives etc. They use market mechanisms and tools which regulate the market so that you do not end up polluting the environment or congest the roads. We take only one side of the ideas from the developed countries. You must look at how they regulate their markets, how they ensure discipline and order. We do only one side of the thing and we do not do the other side. The

Municipalities or Corporations in Australia, fine you if you are not maintaining the lawn in front of your house. You have to maintain it in public interest. If you do not do it you get a notice from the Municipality and you are in trouble. Here nothing we can manage. Many of these things can be traced to introducing something on which you have no controls.

Another, a little different thing is our seafood exporters want to get the best price possible for exports. We want export subsidy, fuel subsidy, import Out Board Motors at cheapest prices. But they do not want any import of fish. They want freedom to impcrt all inputs they want. If you say we feel our economy cannot be exposed to the global competition. We shall be self-sufficient. That sounds logical. You can't go to the global community and put up this one-sided deal. You must have a consistent logic. I find many of the anti-globalization arguments are based on this kind of one-sided deal. I am ready to respect those who critique globalization with a consistent logic.

Q: Specifically, what kind of control mechanisms are you talking about? Can you cite an example from the fishery?

Let met tell you this. Our institutions are doing deep sea fish survey. Yes, data is important to be able to manage the fishery. But there is no fishery management in place. You are spending crores of rupees on vessels to do survey. To use data and manage fishery there is no mechanism in place. What is the point in collecting the data? All that they can say from that data is: resource increased or resource decreased. Okay, you are saying there is 200 tonnes of tuna in the exclusive economic zone of the Indian Ocean. How does it help my fisherman in Nagapattinam to get a good catch? My question is: what are you doing with that data? If that data is not useful at the micro-level, what is the use of that data? These are some of the disconnects in our system which we have to rectify. At first we have to set our home in order. And globalization is only incidental to that.

Q: What can you say as opportunity due to globalization that we can make use of?

There is nobody producing fish cheaper than we do that they can be sold in the Indian market, at the tariff levels existing. The reality as of now is, there is no significant import of seafood into India. Our seafood processing units in Cochin, they are now importing certain varieties of fish to Cochin, reprocess, pack and export them. Similarly, Quilon is the cashew capital of the world. We have huge infrastructure for cashew processing. They import cashew from East African countries also, process and export them. There is every possibility for Cochin to emerge as the fish processing hub if we play our cards properly. But we must be alert enough to understand at what stage it affects the local markets and local producers. There are several opportunities we can identify.

Q: What would you say are the threats to fisheries sector due to globalization?

One of the principles of global trading is that you cannot introduce a discriminatory kind of restriction for your local products and for a similar product from a foreign country. The western countries are able to use non-tariff barriers such as sanitary and phyto-sanitary measures to protect their local markets. We do not have phyto-sanitary measures at the local markets here. Then how are you going to say that it does not confirm to our standards. This is one of the reasons why the Government is bringing in regulations in several sectors. Whether we implement them or not, we can at least show it to foreign competitors that we do have sanitary regulations. It has been internationally agreed that you have to bring down tariffs. So, if you really want to block you have to introduce only non-tariff barriers. How to introduce non-tariff barriers in a non-discriminatory manner is the challenge now. I am still of the opinion that the imports of seafood will not be a threat to our domestic market.

Q: How do you react to Panchayats being promoted as local institutions to take on the challenges brought about by globalization?

In a place like Andamans, where higher tiers are not developed to the required level, Panchayats are really doing wonders and people have accepted Panchayats as an institutions to solve their problems. For the first time in the history of Andaman, thousands of people have gone and demonstrated to the extent that police had to use tear gas to keep the situation under control. This was against the dissatisfaction of people on the Tsunami Rehabilitation Housing Programme in Andamans. The interesting thing about it was the leadership was provided by the local Panchayats in Andamans. They are working as genuine people's organization. Panchayats have become the best source to provide leadership in Andamans. We have to be realistic, *de facto* what will work where, instead of going for a straight jacketed approach that Panchayat will solve all the problems. If Panchayats can do it let them do it. But, I would argue for non-stereotyped, non-standardized, non-straight-jacketed approach. You will have to look at multiple institutions to satisfy different areas and sectors.

We need to be a little flexible in identifying who all can play the potential actors when it comes to facing globalization, instead of shutting up all other options, as if Panchayat is the panacea. If the effort to build up that institution itself is so high, is my agenda capacity-building of Panchayats or challenging globalization. My critique of the Panchayati Raj System is governance in India or constitution based approach has been a kind of standard and uniform approach which in my opinion shall not work in India for the kind of diversity we have here. It is not taking into account the *de facto* systems of people.

12

Chandrika Sharma

Executive Secretary
International Collective in Support of Fish Workers (ICSF)
Chennai

Fishing operations have, over time, became more capital-and technology-intensive and fish production has increased. However, there is need to review this pattern of growth in order to find out who is actually benefiting. Is it the input suppliers—oil companies, engine manufacturers—and exporters, or is it the fishing community?

Q: What would you say are the major changes that are taking place in Tami Nadu after globalization of Indian Economy?

Fisheries has always, in a sense, been a globalized sector, as there has always been the imperative to sell. Trawling for shrimp, including in Tamil Nadu, for example, was promoted since the early 1980s, given the high demand for shrimp in the world market. Unregulated exploitation of shrimp for exports has led to higher pressure on resources. There is a clear link between high export demand and over-exploitation of resources, particularly in the absence of effective management and regulation.

What has really changed in recent years with the liberalization of the Indian economy and the quest for economic growth, is the higher pressure on the coasts. While earlier fisheries was perhaps the main user of coastal and marine resources, today there is pressure from tourism, urban growth, ports and harbours and the oil industry, on the one hand, and from conservation imperatives on the other. The fisheries sector is also being affected by decisions taken at the international level, such as through World Trade Organization (WTO) agreements and decisions under various International Conventions (CITES, CBD...).

Q: How do you think the life and conditions of the small-scale fishworkers have changed due to technology and capital intensity in fisheries?

As competition over and pressure on resources has increased, fishing operations have tended to become more capital-and technology-intensive. To some extent this trend has been supported by the State, such as through schemes promoting motorization and mechanizations. This has also meant that there is a trend towards centralization of landings and bigger catches. This has also, in a way, disrupted some of the traditional patterns. There are harbours, large landings, merchants, traders, exporters etc. instead of small and diversified landings. This has often meant that women, who were an integral part of the chain earlier, are being sidelined. This means that half of the community is being left out. Women have little access to capital, and this has meant losing access to the fish, or at least to the higher value species with higher profit margins. Higher volumes and values are more in the hands of the merchants, traders and exporters now, who are controlling the dynamics at the harbours and fish landing centres. This whole pattern of development requires review. If women are ousted from the sector, the well-being of the community is affected, even if the incomes of the fishermen go up marginally.

Q: You mentioned about reviewing this model of development in the coastal villages. Can you elaborate further about it?

Fishing operations today depend on high cost, often imported inputs, such as engines, gear, fuel etc. The cost of inputs is increasing even though production is not increasing at the same pace (given the limits of the resource base), with the result that the net profit to the fishermen is declining. An important question to ask who is benefiting? Is it the oil companies? Is it the engine suppliers? Is it the fishing community? There is a need to review this pattern of development and to discuss what is needed to better manage resources for better livelihoods of those who actually depend on fisheries for a living.

Q: Development in other sectors affect fisheries? How?

Developments in other sectors are increasingly impacting the fisheries sector. Today, on the coast there is large industry, urban growth, tourism, ports, the oil industry, intensive aquaculture etc. The space left for fisheries and for fishing communities is being squeezed—at one level there are the pressures of economic growth, and at another, conservationists fighting for protected areas. So, coasts are increasingly becoming contested territories. Earlier fishing communities were the only ones on the coast, now there are so many others and communities have to compete with each one of them for space for housing and for fishing and related activities. At the same time the relative power of the fisheries sector *vis-à-vis* all these other high-profile economic activities is certainly low, especially with the emphasis on liberalizing the economy and promoting economic growth.

Another big problem for the fisheries sector is that of pollution—the sea is increasingly being used as a dump for all kinds of wastes. There is need to have policies that protect small-scale fishing communities and their livelihoods in this larger context.

Talking in terms of trade, do you see we have opportunities to gain from, which they say would ultimately percolate down to the fishermen or farmers whoever is at the bottom most rung?

Small-scale fishermen face various barriers in accessing export markets and it is generally felt that WTO disciplines primarily benefit the rich countries. It is difficult, for example, for small-scale fishermen to meet the stringent sanitary standards imposed by the Western world. Non-tariff measures are undoubtedly a significant bottleneck in accessing markets of rich countries. In such a context it is difficult to see how export trade can be of much benefit to small-scale fishermen.

Has economic globalization benefited fishing communities? Ultimately, the proof of the pudding is in eating. We need to ask whether there have been concrete improvements in the quality of life of our fishing communities in terms of basic services such as health, distribution of essential commodities, basic and higher education etc. In today's context of economic globalization the poor in India, including in fishing communities, do not seem to be better off. Why otherwise would thousands of farmers commit suicide?

Q: You mentioned about the resources being depleted unmindful of the potential. How about the aid that came, in the form of funds and technology, after Tsunami? Has it been a reason for this?

One can say that the aid that came after Tsunami has caused several-fold increase in the number of boats in the coastal areas. However, one still needs to know how many of these boats are actually fishing, particularly given the indifferent quality of some of the boats provided. Many of the newer boats may not be fishing at all, particularly where the economics do not work out. High costs of fuel and other inputs is a clear deterrent. Fishermen may prefer not to fish themselves, but to work as crew on another boat, even if they have their own boats.

Q: Do you think Panchayats can play any vital role in facing the challenges and making use of the opportunities, if any brought about by globalization?

While decentralization offers tremendous potential, this necessarily has to be a slow process. There is need to invest in capacity-building of Panchayats and local governance structures. At the same time there is need to take cognizance of existing traditional governance structures, such as the fishing community-level traditional Panchayats in Tamil Nadu. Elected Panchayats will need to work with existing structures.

In the case of fisheries the characteristics of the resource itself, and the fact that stocks are often shared, is also important. There is need for local bodies to work across space and to evolve nested management structures, including within and across States. In the case of stocks like tuna, which is shared between countries, there is a need for different kinds of management structures.

13

Pradeep Sukumar

Assistant Secretary
Planters Association of Tamil Nadu (PAT)
Coimbatore

> *"Globalization is like tying your hands at the back and asking you to fight. The law in this country does not allow me to rationalize my workforce, I cannot be demanding in labour productivity, and I am expected to provide to the labourers everything that a Village Panchayat should provide. How do you expect me to produce at competitive prices and face globalization?"*

Q: We hear that the Indian Tea Industry is undergoing a difficult time in the wake of liberalization. If it's true would you explain what's actually happening?

It is true that the Indian Tea Industry is undergoing a difficult time for almost ten years now. The whole thing boils down to 'price and cost of production', and you will understand why I say so, in the course of our discussion. Before 1998, we were totally dependent on the Russian Market. It was barter kind of a trade. They used to supply us armaments and other equipments, and we used to supply them commodities like tea. It was a very secure market. The South India was totally dependent on the USSR market. In the mid-90s after the USSR collapsed, they also started going for free market economy, regulate their Ruble, trade in hot currency etc. So, why should they purchase tea from India alone? They wanted to trade with us on more commercial terms. Simultaneously countries like Indonesia, Vietnam, Kenya, and Sri Lanka all came up very fast, and became our competitors.

Lots of tea from Sri Lanka and Vietnam started coming into Indian markets. Already there is a surplus in the internal market in India. The arrival of additional quantity created a glut in the market. So, buyers are quoting lower and lower prices. We are put in a desperate position. This year, to some extent, we are okay.

Q: Do you say that tea from countries like Sri Lanka have an edge over Indian tea?

One big difference at that time and to a great extent even now is that we produce only bulk teas and not pocket teas and all that. We are only selling tea 'as commodities' whereas they were value adding them by adding flavour etc., and sold them 'as products'—often branded products. Naturally they got a premium price on their teas. They could ship their tea straight to a super market as a product. It was known as 'Ceylon Tea'. Sri Lanka has actually captured the high end of the market, which we failed to do. The lead in the export market gives them a good margin. What happened ultimately was we have lost our secure market. The internal market is controlled by north Indian producers. Apart from promoting their teas as a product another big difference is in the price. When teas from several countries land in the marketplace, we find that the price of Indian tea is higher.

Q: Can you elaborate why is our price higher than that of the competitor-countries?

One of the reasons for the price of our teas being higher is that it changes so many hands, and I am not very sure if it changes so many hands in other countries—brokers, traders, agents, large wholesalers, distributors, and so on. The cost goes up at every hand. Then again we have cost incurred in blending, packing, tax element, wages and salaries, social benefits to workers, advertisement, transport, retail margin etc. So everything built into that it becomes not less than Rs. 90-100. All these add to the cost.

As planters we have done analysis on the cost of production, and found that 55-60 per cent of the cost of production is incurred in the form of wages, and other statutory benefits offered to the labourers.

Q: Are you taking any measures to bring down the cost of production?

Our fundamental problem is that nearly 60 per cent of our cost of production is labour. With that kind of a cost of production, we will never be able to compete with Vietnam or Indonesia where cost is only about 25-30 per cent of what we incur here. As per the Plantation Labour Act, we are supposed to provide all facilities to the workers. Free education, free housing, free water supply, free crèche facilities, everything is free. Almost what a Village Panchayat should do we are expected to do. Everything costs money. All these add upto cost of production. In 2002 we thought we have reached a breaking point. It was a crucial time we had to make some decision regarding the labour cost. Other cost elements such as taxes, electricity etc. are beyond your control. The only area you really have control over is your labour cost. Experts we consulted reported that we should be able to cut down at least 10-15 per cent on the labour cost.

So we issued notice changing the service conditions. We said we can afford to pay only the minimum wages prescribed by the Government. We were paying Rs. 77 then. If it has to be sustainable it can be a maximum of Rs. 60 a day. Otherwise with the kind of competition posed by Sri Lanka and other countries, it is cheaper to import tea rather than producing here. It has happened in Kerala, about 35 companies have closed down not being able to meet the escalating labour cost and the competition from outside. We do not want such situation to develop here. Instead of having no work at all, we can go ahead with a reduced wage. The unions agreed to Rs. 72. The Government said if you are able to settle between yourselves we would not interfere. Then wages was brought down to Rs. 72 per day.

When I say Rs. 72 you must add at least another Rs. 72 towards housing, water, crèche, medical facility, paid holidays and so on.

Q: **What is your experience with the e-auction system? Does it bring in real competition so that the planters benefit which in turn might reflect in the service conditions of labourers?**

E-auction is like share trading. You can do the trading from your home through internet. If e-auction system operated well there will be more buyers and more competition. Then we shall get better price. But what happens if all these buyers form a cartel. They decide what should be the price. Because there is a legal compulsion that 70 per cent of the made-tea should be sold only through auction centres. It is all the same sellers, same buyers, same brokers. They can form a cartel and quietly dictate prices for various qualities of tea. If you are talking of globalization it should be the same for everybody. The law necessitates me to go to the auction centre even if somebody is ready to pay me a higher price outside the auction system. Later, the Government reduced it to 70 per cent from 85 per cent. So, we are now allowed to sell outside the auction system also. It is open now. All said and done, the Industry is such that we all send to the auction centres only because it is safe. If it is really implemented in full measure it would be beneficial. The demand now is more for orthodox variety of tea. The price goes with quality. In India 80-90 per cent of the tea we produce are CTC (crush, tear and curl) variety which is meant for the low-end market, whereas the world trend now is in favour of orthodox variety—the high end variety.

Q: **Given the trends you are working with what is your impression about globalization?**

Globalization is just like tying your hands and asking you to fight. You can't tie my hands at the back and say you go and fight. Suppose you cannot rationalize your work force, you cannot retrench your staff, you cannot change your productivity, and you cannot change anything, especially in a labour oriented industry, how do you expect me to face globalization? If laws do not permit any of these the planters either tend to violate the law or close down. That's why tea gardens are just being closed down. They have all just abandoned and left. Ultimately, it is the workers who will suffer. If the return on investment is going to be negative, who will want to continue in such a business? The projection now is that there is no future for this kind of large corporate run tea estates. What will happen in the bargain is that organized industry will collapse. If we have to face globalization, let's face it in the way it requires.

Q: The strategies you want to put in place to be able to face globalization?

We are in a situation where we have to produce the maximum out of the minimum. If we are using one unit of electricity, we try to bring out the maximum possible production out of it. If we are employing 100 labourers, we ensure the maximum labour productivity is achieved. We have increased the task levels. Labour productivity level has been increased. Incentives have also been increased so that people who really want to work will get the money. There were days when we used to shut our eyes to those who while away the time. But, now for each deployment of worker we are being very careful.

I should be able to contract out to somebody else. I should be allowed to outsource the work. My permanent labour demands over Rs. 77 a day plus all the other benefits. Whereas I can get it done by a temporary worker paying Rs. 75 and no other benefits. The Plantation Labour Act and the Industrial Dispute Act would not allow me to do this. Then how do I bring down cost of production and compete in the global market. All the other industries are allowed to outsource their functions. We are not allowed to do that. We can give contract to our own workers. You do it for us. We shall give you all support like fertilizers, equipments, guidance etc. You take the tea estate on lease. These are new management models we are thinking to be able to face globalization.

14

Thiru N. Rangaswamy Reddy

Deputy Director (Extension)
Coffee Board, Coimbatore

"Almost 98 per cent of the coffee growers in India are small growers with less than 10 acres. They are contented with the farm-gate price, and they cannot be bothered to look beyond that. Unless they all unite, and understand what international coffee standards are, it's going to be tough."

Q: What is the major change that has taken place in the Indian Coffee Industry in the wake of globalization?

Until the year 1993 the Coffee Board, under the Ministry of Commerce and Industry of the Government, had the monopoly of handling coffee market in India single handedly. Marketing was a major activity of the Coffee Board. We used to get about Rs. 400 crores from the RBI as OD for marketing related operations and used to redistribute sale proceeds to the growers. After the free-trade policy came into being, the growers were allowed to sell upto 70 per cent of their harvest in any open market they choose to. It means it was enough if they sold about 30 per cent through the Coffee Board. After a couple of years, this was made 90:10 and after 1995 it is completely free. The Government (i.e. Coffee Board) is not in the marketing scene any more. It has been made completely private, free and open. Marketing wing has been closed down and to that extent VRS has been implemented to reduce staff at the Coffee Board.

Q: Can you tell the circumstances that led to the Government of India to make a decision that Coffee Board need not involve in marketing of coffee and that it can be free and open?

For any economy it is dangerous to have a monopoly, may be this is one reason. Centrally controlled monopoly would not really help. There should be multi-channel. You provide options the growers can choose from. This is a concept favoured by the open market policy. Secondly, some of the studies conducted by the Government have shown that the marketing expenditure is so much with the Coffee Board. For many of the MNCs in the Coffee Sector, Nestle for example, their marketing expenditures are about 3 per cent of their turnover. But for the Coffee Board it was upto 20 per cent of the turnover. But then you must understand that if you are aiming at small growers your marketing expenditures bound to increase. When we discuss marketing you need to add upto the cost of procurement as well. Thirdly, the produce comes for 3 months and we need to structure the distribution for 12 months. It means the commodity remains in your hands for quite a few months before being converted into cash. In the process, your money is locked in the form of inventory where you lose on the interest you would, otherwise, be earning. All these add upto the total marketing cost. You cannot avoid marketing expenses. May be, this was found unintelligible. So, now the Board is not involved in marketing.

Q: What is the arrangement for marketing now?

As I told you already, now, the market is open and free. In the open market system, for whom a buyer is purchasing and to whom he would sell he does not have to reveal. There are international prices that get uploaded on the Internet. You get coffee price at New York, and London at the click of a mouse. An Inter-governmental organization, which speaks for both producers and consumers, called ICO (International Coffee Organization), does this function. This organization develops political solutions and coffee policy for several governments world over. If a farmer wanted to know the day's coffee price (of any variety) at Thandikudi in Dindigul, he is expected to browse the web and find out the price uploaded by the ICO. The Tatas do it; your local Narasu's Coffee does it, but unfortunately my small farmer is a little scared of the computers. He understands storehouse rates better than the computer mouse. So, he is contented with selling his produce at the farm-gate price.

Q: Can you tell some of the changes that have taken place across countries, which have a bearing on Indian Coffee Industry?

One of the major problems with coffee or any product for that matter is over production, creating a wide demand-supply disparity. Say, for example, the world's coffee production was 130 million bags and the world's consumption was 100 million bags. In that scenario naturally the growers must get a fair return. The prices would be sustainable to the growers. Suppose many farmers become over-ambitious and start producing coffee taking into consideration the fact that coffee is a marketable commodity and it has export potentials as well, then it creates a glut in the market. It has sometimes become global glut as well. The market conditions pull down the prices so badly that it becomes completely non-remunerative. In the past 10-15 years every country started growing coffee. Even Chinese, who until a few years ago have not tasted coffee at all, are also starting to cultivate coffee next to Tibet. Brazil and Vietnam, big players in coffee business, have expanded the area and have gone very vigorously. Whereas India is going very slowly, not doubling up the production. India has never been a major player on coffee front. Our share to the world coffee trade is hardly 4 per cent.

Q: In your opinion, bearing in mind the globalization context, what strengths and what limitations, do you say, the Indian coffee industry has?

Growers like Tata Coffee, Hindustan Levers, and Manjushree Coffee have realized and have the knowledge of the world trade and world's trends. For example, the Tata Coffee has acquired the EOC (Eight O'clock Coffee Company) in the US recently. EOC has about 60 per cent of the US population as his customers. So, Tata's coffee production from India would find a confirmed market in the US. There are certain sectors called Specially Coffee Association (SCA). We have SCA America, SCA India etc. who have established tie-ups and commodity/product flows. In such arrangements transparency is completely absent. It all takes place under a veil. So, the big players are safe. Only my small growers are helpless and the fact is that they make the major chunk of Indian Coffee Industry. May be, our small growers can try to catch hold of the customers that the Tata's might not be able to cater to, because of their concentration in making a presence in the foreign market. With regard to limitation I must mention about the size of land holdings. Most of the holdings are small say, less than 2 acres. Subdivision and fragmentation render it smaller again year after year making it economically unviable. They do not get into grips with the market trends.

Q: Major portion of the coffee plantations belong to the small growers, and the free market economy is found to be unfavourbale to them, what is the Government doing about it?

The Government is trying to see that we measure upto the international standards supporting the Small Growers especially through extension and research. Grants are made available for infrastructure development like construction of godowns, purchase of machineries, technology up-gradation, training in quality up-gradation etc. Geographical Indication system is another patent type of thing, the Government is doing for protecting the uniqueness of some of our coffee varieties such as monsoon Malabar coffee, Coorg coffee etc. These are domestic preparedness the Government is attempting. There are also Agricultural Market Committees and Agricultural Marketing Cooperatives that provide infrastructure to store produces. But not many producers go there. One problem is lack of continuity of policies and inconsistency in offering support. It upsets the farm produces and the farmers. The simple reason for lack of continuity is that a given scheme was introduced when my rival party was in power, so I must see that this scheme dies down.

Q: What are your suggestions in order to make the Small Growers benefit from the globalized market environment?

The growers have to unite. You give them a package and say these are the world standards. Tell them that if you want to make your presence in the world market, adhere to these standards and go for marketing. You can go for contract farming, collective farming, cooperative farming etc. If he is happy with the price he is getting at the farm-gate, what you and I can do to help him. All other countries view India as a very good marketplace taking into account the magnitude of the population. Our small growers do not know how to cash in on his produce. Without preparing the growers to the level of producing quality coffee to compete in open and international markets when we open up it might collapse. Those who are knowledgeable and alert make use of liberalization, and they are in fact happy about open market policy. But to make all the small growers associate and work in a united manner is the real challenge. First of all, we need to teach our small grower to look beyond his farm-gate.

15

V. Jeevanantham

President, Tamil Nadu Green Movement, Erode

> *"To get independence we had to fight for more than 200 years. Likewise, in order to give a human face to capitalistic globalization we will have to fight for another 100 years which may be termed as second war for independence."*

Q: What do you say about the emergence of globalization process?

Globalization is not new to us. It was in practice since long years. In ancient period, traders from Tamil Nadu through their contact with Arab countries exported many items to the erstwhile underdeveloped European countries. In fact, Europe has developed only in the past 400 years after Industrial Revolution. They woke up only after the invention of steam engine. Before that, it is not an exaggeration to say, all the required materials for the European countries were supplied by Eastern Countries like India, China and Egypt. So, we only have initiated the process of globalization. Cardamom, cloves and clothes (Dakha Muslin) were exported by us. We only started the International University in the world for the first time in Nalanda, Taksha Shila, and Kanchipuram etc.

Q: What do you say about the globalization in practice now?

Now, Globalization is against us. Exchange of goods depending upon the needs of both side is the morality of trade. Sharing excess goods with the rest of the world and *vice versa* are ethics of trade. The emergence of capitalism after the industrial revolution changed this situation and led to the accumulation of profit and wealth in the hands of few people and left others to suffer from poverty. It resulted in a situation which is against the humanity. Mass production of capitalist industries have forced them to find new markets and expand their exploitation leaving many to strive and few to thrive because of capitalism. Now, we are not fighting against globalization; we are against the tendency of capitalism in the globalization process which created corporate, multinationals who focusing on the welfare of few rich alone. The capitalist face of global trade is more greedy and cruel. Now, the necessity has come to replace the face of capitalism with humanitarianism in the globalisation. It is essential for the healthy future of our planet and people.

Q: You spoke about the capitalistic globalization. Can you elaborate a little more about its nature, with real-life examples?

India is not against globalized trade. It shared its knowledge with the world countries. Capitalism believes that development cannot be achieved without adopting technology. But MNCs are not ready to come forward to share their knowledge on technology with poor countries. But they are coming here to exploit our water resources and make profit out of it. While we welcome technologies at the same time, it should not lead to retrenching the employment opportunities. Human labour should be prioritized in a thickly populated country like ours. Mechanization should not replace the human hands to a greater extent. Where the population is thin in Europe, mechanization could be the need. But, our government didn't realize that we have 200 crores of hands are available in India to do work. Development should take place for the betterment of people. It should not devastate their life. Technologies threw the people away and kept machines in their places. This leads to unemployment in poor countries. What is going to be the outcome of creating

Special Economic Zone? By investing thousands of crores, acquisition of hundreds of hectares of land from farmers, it is going to provide employment opportunity only to few thousand people. That few knowledgeable/skilled persons who get employment are not going to be the people of the soil. For this our government is prepared to sacrifice its tax income and people's welfare.

Q: What are all the measures to be taken to meet the challenges of the capitalistic globalization?

All of a sudden it is not possible to change the aggressive profit oriented capitalistic globalization. It has got deep rooted in this present day uni-polar world. It can be only changed slowly by the united struggles of all those affected by it. Further its impact is like a cancer which may require a most aggressive correction. Similarly more devoted strategies should be adopted to change the face of capitalistic globalization and its effect. Latin American countries which adopted and experimented globalization 30 years ago, has started rejecting it. Aware of change is visible there. So we need not wait for another 30 years to revolt. Indian and developing countries instead of dwelling the prosperity dreams should immediately form the Latin American countries to defeat capitalists' greed.

Q: Do you say that war and globalization are like Siamese Twins?

War is always the tool of rich and mighty. Poor are not benefited by war; rather they are the worst affected by war. Why does our country want foreign exchange? Why we need the loan from World Bank and IMF? One-third of our budget allocation goes to military, and then the one-third for government salary and expenses. Only one-third goes to developmental works. If we could cut down our military expenses and we take up more hunger alleviation works. We have to buy weapons, mostly from US and other European countries. Our budget allocation, loan from World Bank mostly spent for this and to pay the interest for the loan. If we could create cordial relationship with our neighbours, we need not surrender ourselves to the dictatorship of West dominated globalization.

Q: You hope the defeat of present globalization is certain, can you explain this?

The nature belongs to all of us not those few. They may have all monitory and intellectual support to further their greed. When it crosses the boundaries, the reverse will happen. When nature reacts against its exploitation, the consequences will be unimaginable. What has happened to dinosaurs which ruled the whole earth even before the mankind came into this stage. Where are they? We have just fossil to remind their existence. Latin America which adopted this economy is now turning back. We need not waste our life if we join them the defeat of greed capitalism is inevitable. West *vs* Rest is the battle ground to defeat globalization. Our country can progress well if it could follow Gandhian principles. "To get independence we had to fight for more than 200 years, likewise we have to fight for another 100 years which may be termed as second war for independence in order to bring humanitarian face in place of capitalistic globalization process".

Q: What do you say about the role of Panchayati Raj Institutions in it?

The elected representatives do have an important role in this. At ***first,*** if MNCs approach them to acquire their land for setting up their industries or for creating Special Economic Zones, the representative of the panchayat has to analyse the pros and cons of setting up the industry in their land before giving acceptance to them. If it exploits the nature wealth and livelihood of the people, it should not be allowed. Multinationals like Dubond, Sterlite were driven away from Maharashtra and Goa by vigilant village panchayats. But they have settled down happily in Tamil Nadu.

Secondly, agriculture is considered as the non-profit sector by the farmers. In order to make it as profitable, Panchayat can help the farmers to add value to their products. For example, the cost of ordinary turmeric is Rs. 30 if value addition is done by powdering it can be sold for Rs.100. Government should help agriculture in par with industries.

Thirdly, in order to do value addition to the agri-products, federation can be formed. Subsidies, Bank loans, farmer markets, cold storage, direct purchase by government, eliminating middle men are immediate requirements to protect village economy. For this government has to prepare an Agriculture budget. It has to create an independent, people-friendly organization to protect villages.

Fourthly, measures can be taken to strengthen organic forming. MNCs have an important role in fertilizer industries. Their dominance can be minimized by adopting organic farming. All the subsidies given were siphoned to them. Direct payment of subsidies for organic inputs will benefit farmers.

Fifthly, farmer's association, with the help of Gram Sabha, can help in forming federation rendering technical assistance, services and agri-business.

Lastly, Panchayati Raj Institutions (PRIs) with decentralization of power is the real 'Gram Swaraj'. These PRIs are in a position to protect its farmers, labourers, community property resources like water from exploitation. Panchayats are the basic units of any social change. Strengthening panchayats is strengthening of India, enriching its masses.

16

J. Paul Baskar

Chairman, Peace Trust, Dindigul

> *"The interest of the marginalized should always be protected when a government introduces change in policies— be it liberalization or whatever. When the government fail to insulate this section of the population, and if they got hurt they would turn violent."*

Q: What is your perception about globalization?

Globalisation has made the trade activities fast. The trade agreements favour mostly Multi National Companies (MNCs) and Countries which were benefited in the past during the Colonial period. Globalisation opens up opportunities for everybody in principle. It is only on paper. Practically, developing countries are not capable of taking advantage from the growth process through integration of economic and societies with the technology, goods, services and capital. Capacity levels of these countries are not enough to meet the competition from global level and so these countries are not in a position to accrue benefits from the globalization. Also, these countries don't have adequate support from research organizations. Sometimes, research organizations are mere puppets in the hands of MNCs. Though research organizations claim that they are independent, they are not independent in nature. As a result, local manufacturers are really struggling hard to compete with the foreign products. Labourers, who are working in the private companies, are also affected by liberalized activities.

Q: Specifically, what are all the effects of globalization on working class?

Benefits which come from the globalization is not reaching the grassroots level. It reaches a few families who run the business with large capital. Furthermore, the benefits of globalization are not shared among the communities. The process of globalisation encourages mechanisation. The manufacturing companies, which use machines, provide employment to a handful of workers. These companies do not engage many of the workers. Since, these workers are not organized as a union; they are not able to fight for their wages and other rights related to their working conditions. Eventually, they are not benefited as in the past through government regulations such as provident fund and pension. All these benefits are denied in the name of export and globalization. The company owners are showing interest to export more and earn more profit and developed mindset that labourers should not ask more wage. I think that there is a tendency in some quarters that in export industries nobody should fight with that industry as if they are contributing for the national economy. This type of attitude has been encouraged by the government itself. This attitude would not be of use to make the country as self-reliant. What I want to tell in a nutshell is that the current pace of globalization does not seem to be oriented towards sustainable development and hence, dependency has been created. Self-reliant communities and village raj have become for bidden terminologies.

Q: Could you please elaborate on Sustainability *vs* Globalization?

The community has not been informed about the trade agreement particulars by the government. What would be the outcome from the liberalized policies are not known by the people. They don't know what is going to happen. Without informing the details of trade agreement to the people; it is not easy to get people participate in the management of natural resources. Equity is not possible through this one side approach. In fact, participation, equity and community based natural resource management systems alone would lead the community towards sustainable development. My point is that since the benefits of liberalisaton did not reach even the lower strata of society, the social development couldn't be achieved.

Q: Recently, private developers have been given right to acquire land directly from agricultural land owners and expand the area of the Special Economic Zone (SEZ). What is your opinion on it?

For setting up Special Economic Zone, land has been forcefully taken away, that is what happened at Nandigram in West Bengal. The Central Government has approved to set up many more SEZs in India. Land is the fundamental thing for Indian community as it is the backbone of the livelihood security system for 700 million of our population. For Indian community, land is not only an asset, it is more than that. It has cultural, traditional and emotional value. In this context, there should be a ceiling of land for setting up SEZs. Recent notification issued by the central government has given private developers the right to acquire land directly from agricultural landowners and expand the area of the SEZ. Allowing the private developers to acquire agriculture land directly could enable the sale of large tracts of land and endanger the livelihoods of farmers and agricultural labourers. Actually the private industries must be asked to buy the land at the market prize and in some cases they have to allow the landowners to become shareholders, promoters and Board of Directors wherever possible and take part in business venture in the zone.

Q: How do you and Peace Trust address globalization issues in the present context?

Globalisation is a trend and process now. At *first*, to get benefited from the globalization, information is a vital. As of now, information is with a few people who are able to gain all the benefits from the globalization. Many people are struggling hard to access the information. They should have access to get the information about various opportunities of liberalized policies taken by our government. Information is 'power'. If people are empowered, they can play their role in the development process. In order to inform the people on various socio-economic aspects, our organization has set up a community radio called 'Pasumai FM' through which we create awareness among the people. It acts as a catalyst for the development of rural economy by empowering the people. It enables poor people to gain knowledge through information and equips them to participate in the development process. *Secondly*, people have to be orgainsed into group and they can make the things better for a common goal. ***Finally***, government should change its pro-rich policy. The problems brought out by globalization cannot be tackled without changing the policy. Our government is providing several concessions for rich to become richer. Industry interests are duly taken care through its liberalized policies. It should not forget that poor people are the largest number, if they are not given justice, they will not wait for justice in democracy.

Q: What do you want to say, if the interests of the marginalized are not taken care properly?

Tamil Nadu is one of the leading states in attracting Foreign Direct Investment (FDI). People say Tamil Nadu is the State which attracts investment at the highest level in the whole of Asian Region while attracting foreign direct investment Tamil Nadu Government should not forget the largest marginalized section of people. The interests of this section should always be protected when the government is implementing the liberalized policies. If the government does not take care of the interests of these marginalized section, this section will not wait. A few political parties are providing non-violent articulation for poor and small farmers and campaigning against the entry of private companies in retail business. Now-a-days, people are not hesitated to fight for demanding basic necessities in some places. For example, when Vaigai river water is given to the people of Dindigul city and denying the right of one way side village (for example, Michal Palayam), the village people will not passively watch and wait. When they need water, they will break the water pipeline. Nobody can stop them. Authorities cannot do anything if the people organized into large number. They have to negotiate with the people. I forecast such things will continue to happen if their interests are not protected by the government. Once again, I want to stress that the liberalized policy should be accompanied with pro-poor approach. That is the only answer to the present crisis.

17

S. Muthukumaran

Former Vice-Chancellor
Bharathidasan University, Tiruchirapalli

> *You procure one litre of milk for Rs.10, and add half a litre of water to it. You resell it at Rs.12 a litre. How much profit do you make? is the kind of mathematics taught to children in today's mathematics classes. What ethics are you teaching your children? Money is everything and you make money anyway?*

Q: Can you share with the readers of Global and Local your impression of 'Education For All'?

Education for all has been on the development agenda ever since India became independent. It [EFA] used to find place with varied scope and significance from time to time because literacy was, and still is being recognized as a pre-condition to change the conditions of living of poor people. There was a time we had systems like Common School System, and the neighbourhood school system etc. Talking about 'Education for all', we obviously understand the implication that quantity in enrolment and completion rate. But, quality aspect of education remains silent. It is only of late, the Government of Tamil Nadu has started making specificities like *'samacheer Kalvi'* meaning education for all in the quantitative sense of the expression, and *'seeranakalvi'* meaning 'quality education'.

Q: What do they mean when they say 'quality education'?

The concept of education for all presupposes the availability of equally good quality education to every child.

Identical syllabus and text books, per se do not provide quality education. Only if the syllabi, textbooks, facilities for teaching learning process including the quality and number of teachers, facilities for extracurricular activities and everything connected with learning are of a good quality and appropriate learner, it can be said that quality education is made available to every child. But, today the trend is if children at primary level are able to talk a little bit of broken English, then it is considered that that school is imparting quality education—as if anything in the vernacular (Tamil) is inferior. This is sad.

Q: What have you to say about language as medium of instruction?

It is generally accepted that the main subjects of study in schools include languages, mathematics, sciences and social sciences. The first duty of a primary school teacher must be to teach the mother tongue well. Teaching of the state language if the mother tongue of the child is different from the state language should be the next most important duty. Teaching of any other language has to wait until the child has acquired minimum competencies in the mother tongue and in the state language. The country adopted some years ago, a three language formula. In the words of Ramamurthi Committee, the three-language formula includes the study of a modern Indian language, preferably one of the southern languages, apart from Hindi and English in Hindi speaking states, and of Hindi along with the state language and English in the non-Hindi speaking states. Tamil Nadu rejected this formula and adopted a two-language formula which includes compulsory study of English and Tamil or any modern Indian language. This paved way for one permanently residing in Tamil Nadu not studying Tamil, yet passing all the standards and even getting a degree. In due course, this was considered anachronistic and in 2006, the state government issued a new order by which it made study of Tamil compulsory in the schools in Tamil Nadu. The idea behind making every child to learn two or three languages was that every child in this country would grow up with proficiency in the state language and the official language of the country, i.e. Hindi and English. In fact, The National Curriculum Framework—2005 has observed: A student may be allowed to 'pass without English' if an alternative route for English certification can be provided outside the regular school curriculum. I would endorse this idea. It is not fair you detain a student just because he has not acquired a foreign language.

Q: What is your impression about the new ABL method of teaching adopted in schools?

In my opinion, there can be no universal method of teaching. As the grasping power, competence and exposure levels of children vary, there can be no uniform methodology to teach. You cannot prescribe a single methodology and say that it should be adopted state-wide. ABL is a method of teaching. But, you cannot say that it is applicable to all the schools and to all the children. Before ABL, they were talking about 'play way method of teaching' and I do not know what is happening about it now.

I would suggest that you teach all teaching methodology to the teachers, and leave it to the discretion of the teacher, to choose which method he/she thinks would best suit the circumstances, and the competence level of the children. Otherwise, at least it can be left to the school, or to a Panchayat Union, or at the most to a district level. Methodology is one and content is another. I mean the morality or the space provided for moral education content is reducing which is a matter of concern.

Q: Do you think the space provided for moral education can be more, given the speed at which knowledge is generated today, and the need to learn more and more to become competent in the job market?

Today, both the parents are working. They have no time to teach any morality to children. Only the school should plan teaching morality. Good things and morality can be taught in any subject. For example, you procure one litre of milk for Rs. 10, and add half a litre of water to it. You resell it at Rs. 12 a litre. How much profit do you make? is the kind of mathematics taught to children in today's mathematics classes. What ethics in business are you teaching your children?

Q: Under SSA, it is said Local Self-Governments have a significant role to play with local schools. What is your impression about it?

It is a good thing that Panchayats work hand in hand with local schools. It is also true that SSA has a feature called Village Education Committee (VEC) that is subsidiary of the Local Self-Government. It has powers to decide on the facilities that the local school requires, and ask for funds from the state government. Any new development in the school especially in terms of infrastructure development should be done with the concurrence of the Panchayat only. I have no knowledge of how functional these VECs are. I must visit some Panchayat Union Schools. In fact, the school teachers should be attached to Panchayats—though not the Village Panchayat, at least to the Block Panchayat or District Panchayat. But, it will have several political repercussions and so, people in power would not make such moves.

18

V. Balakrishnan

Convener
Tamil Nadu Primary School Improvement Campaign (Tan-PIC), Chennai

---

> *"The more you are educated, the higher is the propensity to move out of this country. The country that developed them so far so long is not a comfortable place to live any more. Then how do you expect me to take that this education system taught you the right thing."*

Q: As head of an organization 'campaigning for quality primary level education in Tamil Nadu', what is your impression of Primary Education today?

We are concerned of several things pertaining to quality education at primary level in Tamil Nadu starting from quality infrastructure to syllabus and curriculum making. We should realize that this system of education we have today was formulated long ago bearing in mind producing clerks generation. Similarly, the infrastructure plans are almost half a century old. Changes have taken place in the society, and in the educational system and administration. But these changes do not aim at protecting and furthering the local culture, language, and dignity of children etc. People who think sensibly would not feel comfortable with the direction of change in education in general and primary education in particular is taking place today.

Q: We find there are a lot of changes taking place in the educational system, especially at Primary level, after the introduction of SSA. What have you tell about them?

In my opinion, and in the opinion of people who keep observing the development of primary education in the state, there are several things to change. One of them is infrastructure in Union Primary Schools, insist teaching through mother tongue until completion of primary level education or until the children get familiar with the mother tongue/state language. The children may be engaged to take up a foreign language like English only after they know how to read, write and speak in their mother tongue well. Let the private matriculation schools do whatever they think the market demands. But, the government should promote only a culture that is local or ethnic which shows the children the greatness of Tamil culture, language and civilization. For that matter, the state has the responsibility to control even the private matriculation schools at the time of giving state recognition certificates etc.

Q: You asked for change in syllabus and curriculum. What kind of change are these?

The syllabus and curriculum making, as of now, is centralized. It is from the NCERT. We demand this to be decentralized. Perhaps, you have heard of ABL method being implemented in all the primary schools in Tamil Nadu. My question is: do the children know the local festivals, traditions, social norms and mores? Or do they at least know how to talk in their mother tongue without mixing the English language? The teacher should be allowed to prepare lesson plans based on a broad guideline giving importance to self-discovery and local/regional history. I would appreciate if we can develop a system whereby even regional dialects of Tamil is recognized and accepted as medium of education in schools. I doubt if the bookish kind of Tamil is scaring the children away. This bookish Tamil should be replaced with regional dialects of Tamil taking the argument that bookish Tamil is in actuality non-existent.

Q: Do you think all this is possible, talking from the perspective of growth direction the nation is taking—such as change in the socio-political and economic situations in the country and the demands of the market forces, competition in getting seats at the institutions of higher learning etc.?

You want to 'rear' your children for the job market to enable him to proceed to the US or Canada after getting an Engineering degree here. I am talking about developing good citizens and societal change that value this culture and language. You are talking about earning wealth for your family. I am talking at the national interest and in the interest of human well-being without greed. Selling education through the shops called schools have become a lucrative business today. In that order the Union Primary schools are for the marginalized and the poor; the local private schools are for the middle class; the matriculation schools at the city are for the upper middle class; and the rich would go to the international schools at Kodaikanal or Ooty. This is the order today. But, you must know what it results in. Those who completed class ten think that village is not for them to make a living. Those who complete degree courses are bent upon getting a white collar job in the city. Those who complete a professional degree course are after foreign assignment and foreign companies. India is not fit for them to live or work. The country that developed them so far so long is not a comfortable place to live in any more. The more you are educated, the higher is the tendency to move out of this country. Then how do you expect me to take that this education system taught you the right thing. What is happening to common school system and the neighbourhood school system?

Q. What do you think an education system should achieve?

The government has enough money mobilized as property tax in the cities, education cess and so on. Why not provide quality education at primary level. Why not establish common school system and the neighbourhood school system. Implement cross-subsidy plans. Show the children the value of tradition, dignity of labour, and respecting the mother tongue. The education system should help him discover his village, understand his community and the neighbourhood. Let him understand and discover himself before anything else. Getting admission in an Engineering or medical college cannot be the ultimate goal of primary or secondary education. If you take this as the ultimate purpose; minus the one and a half lakh Engineers and doctors produced every year, what are you doing with the rest of the educated youth? The private business persons running educational institutions might try to offer whatever the market demands for money. The market may or may not have any ethics. But there should be ethics in whatever the government does.

